Eloquence and Mere Life

POETS ON POETRY · Donald Hall, General Editor

Alan Williamson

Eloquence and Mere Life

ESSAYS ON THE ART OF POETRY

Ann Arbor
THE UNIVERSITY OF MICHIGAN PRESS

1997   1996   1995   1994   4   3   2   1

A CIP catalogue record for this book is available from the British Library.

ISBN 978-0-472-09568-1 (sqb)

ISBN 978-0-472-06568-4 (pbk)

Preface

I've known poets whose entire loyalty was to the splendor possible in the art, the intensification of language beyond its normal powers that makes a state of being or feeling crash down, like a dazzling wave, on the reader. I've known other poets driven only by an impatience with "poetry," a desire to make it include more of what, in language or experience, strikes them as the "real." But the poets I've loved best, and wanted to write about in prose, are the ones who cannot relinquish either claim, intensity or reality. That way lies surprise, tortuous mediation, that stretching of the bounds of the aesthetic which the philosopher Bernard Bosanquet (in a phrase I owe my friend Jeanne Foster) called "difficult beauty." Such poets can be—usually are—guilty of rough edges. They cannot be guilty of the one aesthetic liking I've never been able to take seriously—the well-made poem, that clicks shut so firmly because so little is contained.

It seems particularly important to talk about such predilections—what one feels separates the "good" from the "best"—at the present time. With more and more people trying to be poets, fewer and fewer publishers willing to take the financial risk, and little agreement—or education—about even the minimal skills that constitute good writing, we face a Babel of coterie standards. Formalists praise form; workshops praise "accessibility" and the avoidance of cliché; others simply make taste in poetry an adjunct to social, political, or pop-psych agendas. The academy has lost interest, and faith, in value judgments between "texts." If the poet-critics do not speak for more elusive, but real, criteria of poetic merit, who will?

All of the poets discussed at any length here seem to me

exemplars of "difficult beauty." The essays that do not deal directly with the question of eloquence and realism tend to deal with other tensions too often made into dualisms: statement and image; form and free verse; political poetry and the value of inwardness. I have divided the essays into three groups. The first deals with Lowell's generation, the poets who set the terms when I was starting out as a writer. (I regret, here, the omission of my recent writings on Jarrell, Ginsberg, and Snyder, which form parts of other, as yet unfinished, projects.) The second section deals with larger, more theoretical issues, and generally takes its examples from farther afield, in time, space, and language. The third section is about "a sense of generation"—the poets I care for most, my own age and younger, and how we seem to have configured ourselves, in relation to the Romantic, as well as the realist, traditions that came to us from the past. Some of these pieces have come, willy-nilly, to be a kind of aesthetic autobiography, which I have tried not to make too self-important.

One decision I made, in the effort to hold this book to a manageable length, was to include no brief or portmanteau reviews. This decision was good, I think, for the general level of thoughtfulness; less so for a sense of the breadth of my taste. I particularly regret the omission of certain writers who are not discussed in other essays, or in my previous books. Some of these are famous—John Logan, Louis Simpson—but the ones who are most on my conscience are the more avant-garde, younger, or less widely appreciated: Clayton Eshleman, Maria Flook, Christopher Gilbert, August Kleinzahler, Jack Marshall, Belle Randall, Gary Soto. My apologies to these writers, whose work remains important to me, and to my sense of the richness of the contemporary scene.

Contents

Contents

I

Robert Lowell

A Reminiscence

I met Robert Lowell when I came to Harvard as a graduate
student in 1964, and, being a little diffident of presenting
myself as a poet, went to take his literature course, called "The
Craft of Poetry." So I saw him for the first time on the tenth
floor of Holyoke Center, his large head silhouetted against its
northern exposure: the Yard; the Victorian brick steeples
aligned toward North Cambridge, like an architectural junk
shop of the ages of faith; and, mainly, pale gray early autumn
sky. It was not unlike the setting he chose to describe in his
own memoir of Sylvia Plath: high places suited him. And his
talk, his reading, that fall seemed to dwell on the paradox of
our consciousness above, but never freely above, its material
nature and end: Hardy remembering his dead wife in her
"original air-blue gown"; Emily Dickinson's "surmise," which,
for Lowell, was not securely "Immortality," but a finite exis-
tence trying to grasp an infinite prospective non-being . . . He
ranked the English Victorians, and put Hardy and Arnold
first; I believe for the syncopated, conversational wrench of
individual pain they gave to the common elegiac cadence of
the age—a combination he himself was then using master-
fully, in poems like "Water," "The Old Flame," "Near the
Ocean." However well I came to know him later, the larger-
than-life image I formed of him at that time never entirely
faded from my mind.

He could be a man of terrible and wonderful moral

Harvard Advocate, November 1979.

impressiveness. Shortly after that course in "The Craft of Poetry" ended, Lyndon Johnson began bombing North Vietnam, and Lowell's refusal to attend the White House Festival of the Arts made the front page of the *New York Times*. The next fall, I heard him read "Central Park" and "Waking Early Sunday Morning" in Sanders Theater, at a benefit for an antiwar organization called Massachusetts PAX:

> Only man thinning out his kind
> sounds through the Sabbath noon, the blind
> swipe of the pruner and his knife
> busy about the tree of life . . .

In the question period, a man—I think a reporter—rose from the second row and said, "You speak in your poem of 'man thinning out his kind.' Do you regard the [largo; all capitals] UNITED STATES OF AMERICA as the agent of this thinning out?" Lowell said, "Don't you?" He let at least a minute go by in total silence, then insisted, "I asked you a question, and I'd like an answer." Another minute of silence; then, his point made, Lowell continued very softly, "I said *man* thinning out his kind; and that's what I meant; and it's going on all around us; and pray God it will stop."

In recent years some people—notably Louis Simpson—have wondered how Lowell, with his pessimism, his pacifist breadth of sympathy, his aversion to sloganeering, could have been a figure of comfort and inspiration to a radical movement. One answer might be the simple contrast between the usual journalistic poem on napalm and the lines I have quoted—a Poundian ideogram allowing the Bible, American defoliation tactics, and that tidy old conservative metaphor of statecraft as gardening to comment on each other by superposition. Another answer might be that Lowell's very ambivalence, his refusal to fall for easy hopes or to relinquish any imaginatively valuable point of view, gave a special meaning to his radical, and even illegal, actions, at a time when others used "complexity" as an excuse to avoid uncomfortable choices. Lowell's mere presence, like Montale's in Fascist Italy, seemed to prove that the best, the living edge, of traditional culture was on the dissenting side. Perhaps his unwilling extremeness—that seemed "to wince at pleasure, / and suffocate for privacy"—had a special appeal in Massachusetts, where students did not burn their draft cards but laid them in the collection plate at the Arlington Street Church, while the congregation sang the words of an earlier Lowell:

> Once to every man and nation comes the moment to decide,
> In the strife of Truth with Falsehood, for the good or evil
> side.

Robert Lowell spent much of his life criticizing the implications of that ancestral absolutism about politics, but one can't help reflecting that he would have been a less interesting and less admirable man if it had not been so deeply ingrained in him; if relativism had been his essence, and not a deliberately cultivated corrective.

His private personality, on the other hand, was genuinely casual, even languorous (and yet still more vivid, I think, in the memory of anyone who knew him well). He preferred to speak in impressions rather than judgments: "One feels that . . ." He carried his large body in a headlong, fumbling way he himself called "fogbound"; and preferred slumped, lounging postures when seated. (He was happiest of all lying full length on a sofa.) He liked to live in a certain amount of disorder; he joked in a poem that the President of Columbia's study after the student takeover was "much like mine left in my hands a month," and once scandalized and delighted a friend by saying that his cat lived "on what she picks up around the house." His talk was counterpointed and qualified by an endless vocabulary of hand gestures—chopping, hovering, smoothing; the hands held crosswise before him and then pushed out to the side, as though separating unruly conglomerated masses; the circling index finger of vertigo and resolution—gestures suggesting a kind of psychomachia latent in the ordinary conversational facts of balance or overstatement, banality or precision.

Perhaps as a kind of escape valve for this inner battle, a

peculiar, teasing, fantasy-laden humor tinged almost everything Lowell said in his last years. I remember my wife telling him about the troubles a friend—a student of Marcuse—had had living in the tightly knit household of her Communist, but none the less traditional, Bengali mother-in-law. Instantly Lowell had Marcuse himself moving into the house, trying to take things in hand, writing a constitution . . . "The mother-in-law would win," was his conclusion. Sometimes the same humor glimmered darkly in his public actions: when asked for a Bicentennial poem, he obliged with one comparing Nixon's antics in his "final days" to the madness of George III. But most of his humor was personal and affectionate, and does not carry well without his voice, which was, to the slight shock of most people meeting him for the first time, Southern: not broad Southern, but the mild, pleasant drawl of Kentucky and Tennessee, where so many of his intimates—Elizabeth Hardwick, Peter Taylor, Allen Tate, Randall Jarrell—had grown up. He had a way of deliberately intensifying that accent's natural purrs and pauses that could set a whole room laughing, even when his joking was at its undergraduate nadir: "The great mystery about Peter [Taylor] . . . is his *age*. . . . Nobody really knows . . . how *old* he is . . ." (And yet, the fact that this unforgettable voice was acquired, largely, from the same friends he teased with it suggests one of the vital contradictions in his character: his relation to others was at once dominating and expansive and curiously, even poignantly, dependent.)

I came to know Lowell better through attending his "office hours" from 1966 to 1968. These office hours were a Harvard institution over many years, but the English department would not tell one exactly when and where they were held; one knew, or one did not. In my day, it was Wednesday morning, from 9:30 to 12:00, in a windowless, cement-block seminar room in Quincy House. Lowell's best undergraduate students came, as did a slightly larger number of graduate students, and some already recognized poets living, or visiting, in the area. In the late 1960s the regulars included—among many others—Jean Valentine, Helen Chasin, Richard Tillinghast, Frank Bidart, Grey Gowrie, Lloyd Schwartz, Courtenay Graham, and James Atlas. Most mornings, we waited tensely—though doing our best, under the influence of the Master's serene lassitude, to conceal it—for our poems to come up and be judged; but occasionally Lowell would read his own work in manuscript, or simply talk, about history, religion, or politics as often as about poetry. (Once a whole morning was spent on Churchill's history of the Second World War, with unorthodox comparisons between its author, Hitler, and Stalin.)

Lowell was a casual teacher, and economized the effort he put into understanding any single student poem; so it's a little hard to pin down why he defined, for me, the only imaginable way of trying to teach "creative writing." He managed to avoid the two easiest, but in some ways most limiting, paths a teacher can take: to be too readily pleased with work that is merely sincere, and does what it sets out to do; or to make the student better by rules, whether the old rules of rhyme, meter, impersonality, or the new rules of whatever style is most in vogue. He made us feel how rarely we touched the hem of truly memorable poetry. He would listen to the student read the poem once, then read it aloud himself, his hand hovering like a divining rod until he reached a particular detail or turn of phrase, then plumping down: "It comes to life here." As often as not he would hand the student back a new poem, constructed on the spot out of the two or three passages that "came to life." If one had the temerity to object—after the manner of well-trained English majors in those days—that certain omitted elements formed a *pattern* with those retained, he would say something like, "If it's there already, why bring it in twice?" Provided that the poem belonged to a style and genre he found sympathetic to begin with, he was often uncannily right as to where the emotional center, the possible originality, lay. He came as near as I can imagine anyone coming to teaching the intuitions—about one's real subject; about diction; about structure—which so often distinguish good, let alone great, poets from journeymen.

This is not to say that he was a perfect teacher. His taste had its rigidities. He was partial to a kind of generic 1960s poem vaguely influenced by his own style in *Life Studies:* a freshly observed detail in every line, but a quiet, everyday, even slightly depressed, tone of voice. Poems influenced by his own high style, or by any hermetic mode, left him deeply ambivalent ("good lines . . ."); he was also unsure how plain poetry could dare to be, in the interests of ascetic truthfulness ("underenergized"). The same conflicts expressed themselves in his judgments of his peers and predecessors: fascinated irresolution over Hart Crane; high praise for poets like Dugan and Snodgrass; gingerliness toward Ginsberg, the Black Mountain School, Ashbery (though he admired *Kaddish,* and had a late change of heart with Ashbery, over "Self-Portrait in a Convex Mirror"). One was not altogether encouraged to argue with these judgments in the classroom; yet in the long run Lowell often showed greater interest in the students who revered him, but disagreed.

It was not always easy to pass from being his student, or his acquaintance, to being his friend (in my own case, real friendship came only after I had left Harvard, when we were, geographically, far apart). He had, and needed, his barriers; his own hypersensitivity mixed badly with the hypersensitivity and self-consciousness his fame evoked in most people who met him. But the other half of the story was the almost inexhaustible pleasure he took in being at leisure with his friends—spending a whole day together, reading each other's new work, taking walks, drinking white wine through dinner, and long after. He showed affection easily and without embarrassment, beginning a letter to an old (male) friend who had been ill, "Well, old dear . . ." He willingly used his own prestige to "throw a lifeline" to others (his own words about Randall Jarrell). I well remember the only long-distance call I ever had from him, which came the day after I had been refused tenure in the English department where I was then teaching. He loved gossip, and liked enlisting others in boyish conspiracies: I remember him regretfully eyeing the empty wine bottles on the table—too near dessert time, with too slow-drinking a party—then whispering to me, "Let's just ask the waiter for another round." Nobody else caught on, until three newly opened full bottles sat in our midst . . . That story came back to me, reading the passage in *Day by Day* where he imagines heaven as

> a sensual table
> with five half-filled bottles of red wine
> set round the hectic carved roast—

and then, even more wonderfully, as "the familiars of a lifetime . . . running together in the rain to mail a single letter."

This is not the time or place to go into what little I know about Lowell's experience of madness. What—beyond his poetry, even—made him a hero to a great many people was the fact that, living in the imminence of an internal chaos that would have wrecked many lives, he so often seemed stronger and not weaker than the normal person: in his steady and enormously ambitious work, which even illness could not interrupt; in his political courage; in the importance he gave to friendship; and in his ability to synthesize harsh truths with deeply felt values. I believe R. D. Laing wrote somewhere that one should wish to be able to see the things a mad person sees, while remaining sane. Lowell would probably have distrusted the romanticism of that statement, but the need constantly to recognize and accommodate the undersides of motives, the irrational theatricalities of the mind, was part of the stature of his character: the swimming balance of a violent man who liked languor, a helpless *voyant* who overvalued realism. (When he was told, once, that smoking pot helped one to see one's own mental states through external things, he replied dryly, "I never had any trouble doing that.")

In his last years—when his life was made a great deal easier by lithium, and breakdowns tended to come mainly in the wake of external crises—he tried, almost as a kind of spiritual exercise, to see his peculiar fate as a mere variant of the generic tragedy, and pleasure, of being human and an individual. A curious, joyful feeling of being—not in the ordinary sense—beside himself, beside his own life, runs through his late poems. I think, particularly, of one of the very best, "Thanks-Offering for Recovery":

> The airy, going house grows small
> tonight, and soft enough to be crumpled up
> like a handkerchief in my hand.

In this detachment, Lowell becomes a kind of Everyman, "the *homme sensuel,* free / to turn my back on the lamp, and work." Later in the poem, he stands beside himself in a more drastic, even grotesque, sense; the story requires retelling. When he was recovering from a breakdown, Elizabeth Bishop sent him, as a get-well present, a Brazilian ex-voto—the replica of the afflicted part of the body which Latin Catholics give to the saint believed responsible for the cure. Too late, Bishop realized to her chagrin that this particular object was specific to "head-injury or migraine." (I can still almost hear Lowell's voice relishing these words, just as he relished his own joke about "Peter's age.") In the poem, the ex-voto becomes, with wonderful ambivalent wit, an emblem of Lowell's problematic specialness, of madness, of the closed-in self-observation and self-recording which apparently grew more unremitting with depression:

> a head holy and unholy,
> tonsured or damaged,
> with gross black charcoaled brows and stern eyes
> frowning as if they had seen the splendor
> times past counting. . . .
> It is all childcraft, especially
> its shallow, chiseled ears,
> crudely healed scars lumped out
> to listen to itself, perhaps, not knowing
> it was made to be given up.
> Goodbye nothing.

It is terrible, no doubt, to come to regard a great part of one's life, spent in pain, as a "nothing"; but it is also freedom . . . In many theologies, it is at the threshold of a beatific vision that one feels that evil is not substantial but merely privative; that the self-conscious self is the "shadow" of a larger universal one. This much is explicit: Lowell has, however shakily or temporarily, escaped the sense that he is merely the self, and plaything, of fate, "created to be given away." The ex-voto—like his autobiographical poetry, though the analogy is never leaned on—has taken his place as scapegoat, allowing him to float free into a dimension, "airy," undefinable, where mere existence is its own purpose and recompense.

Such a serenity and ease seemed to radiate from Lowell, though he talked freely of depression, the last time I saw him, during the great European heat wave of July 1976. Perhaps for that reason, when I try to distinguish these late poems from the poems of loss and determinism in *For the Union Dead,* I think of the distance between Holyoke Center and the scene of our last meeting. The wavering of London under the heat; the floor-through townhouse room, another high place, almost as bare as a classroom, but with a seventeenth-century mounting around the one mirror; and Lowell opening a drawer where a hundred of those family photographs which, in life as in his "Epilogue," he loved so specifically, lay unmounted, rising on each other like waves in the sea.

The Reshaping of "Waking Early Sunday Morning"

The drafts for "Waking Early Sunday Morning" in the Houghton Library at Harvard run to forty-one typed sheets, in the course of which the poem grows from three stanzas to its final length.[1] This is not particularly unusual; Robert Lowell revised, as he once said, "endlessly," and often made superb poems out of unpromising and truncated early drafts, changing and even reversing the things he chose to say as he changed his sense of the pattern they made. What drew me to the drafts of "Waking Early"—when I first saw a sample of them in a memorial exhibition at Houghton—was the way in which they seemed to confirm, as an active force in the actual psychology of composition, certain attitudes toward public subject matter which I had hypothesized from the body of Lowell's finished work in my book, *Pity the Monsters*. One of my hypotheses was that Lowell associated his own more formal high style with political engagement (an association so contrary to most contemporary taste that Louis Simpson has recently argued, in a peculiarly circular manner, that "Waking Early" has to be politically conservative because it is metrical). Lowell regarded both terms of the equation, I believed, with ambivalence, associating them with a surrender to dangerous inward exaltation. But Lowell's old friend Robert Fitzgerald has put this better than I could, speaking, in a memoir written shortly after Lowell's death, of Lowell's tendency to "make a stir" in public:

Agenda, autumn 1980.

The trouble was that sometimes the stir accompanied or worsened into a crisis. After his first grave manic attack in 1949, after his first hospitalization, all concerned grew wary on his behalf, as indeed he did himself, of excitements religious, political, or poetic. He could no longer be a Catholic because, as he told me, it set him on fire. He had to govern his greatness with his illness in mind. *Life Studies* were an early and extreme result of this kind of discipline and scaling down.

My second contention was that Lowell's best public writing made conscious use of these connections, and was linked to his "confessional" writing by an analogy—sometimes tacit, sometimes explicit—between his own experience of madness and the irrationalities in the behavior of statesmen, and in mass psychology.

On a complete reading of the drafts, the development of "Waking Early Sunday Morning" provides remarkable evidence in support of these hypotheses. As first written, "Waking Early" was a poem of hesitation between styles, painfully and explicitly paralleling Lowell's hesitation about the legitimacy of presenting himself as a public figure. There was no mention of Lyndon Johnson, the Vietnam War, or any of the issues that had specifically stirred Lowell to "dreams of power." Gradually, grudgingly, and often by telling associative substitutions of political for private material, "Waking Early" was made over into a public poem; until finally—by the elimination, between magazine and book publication, of two of the first stanzas actually written—all indication that it had ever been essentially a poem about poetry (and, for that matter, a repudiation of grand themes) was suppressed.

Lowell's refusal to attend President Johnson's White House Festival of the Arts in June 1965, in protest against the Vietnam War, was by any standard the biggest "stir" he had created since his conscientious objection in World War II (it made the front page of the *New York Times*). Some years later, in an interview in the *Review,* Lowell confessed to a sense of constraint in the aftermath: "I felt miscast, felt burdened"—one must presume, by the imagined expectations of his audience—"to write on the great theme." In the poem-draft—first three stanzas, then five (see facsimile no. 1)—that appeared in his papers shortly after the festival incident, the sense of temptation and reluctance is clear; but whether Lowell's own explanation, or Robert Fitzgerald's, is more relevant is, I think, open to question.

Lowell's aspirations to influence politics are dismissed in this draft, without specific examination, as megalomaniac "dreams of power," compelling only, it would seem, because other, perhaps better, fulfillments or transcendences (love? art?) have failed. Though the poem is, in fact, carrying out a return to "meter and iambic line," this too is treated—along with "rhetoric" and a more sweeping, "allegoric" generality of content—as so much false gigantism and military macho. The poet seems to feel both a sense of punishable hubris (the word itself appears, in place of "confidence," in a subsequent draft; and Goliath was, after all, cut down by a youthful challenger) and of before-the-fact exhaustion ("I cannot take it"). It is in this context of self-caricature of Lowell the public poet that lines eventually applied to Lyndon Johnson ("sick / of stretching for the rhetoric": "sick / of his ghost-written rhetoric") first enter the poem.

If, on the other hand, "I gave up politics," a wholly different kind of poetry would become possible. The "dregs and dreck"—later both more literal and more obscurely symbolic—here clearly refer to a kind of writing, "more honest" than the grand style because the author himself is not aware of imposing a "purpose": the "phrases buried in conversation" that would, a few years later, become so much the guiding principle of *Notebook;* the meaningless image of the china doorknob that—as Lowell recounted elsewhere—haunted him as he began to write *Life Studies.* Such a principle of composition lies somewhere between realism and the programmatic randomness of action painting. In 1965, at least, Lowell viewed it with a certain wariness. At its extreme, things fall apart; "substance" and "symbol" become irreconcilable opposites; the poet cannot make his material his own by making manifest a latent meaning—as Lowell, in fact, could not in the case of the china doorknob.

I have argued elsewhere that there is a consciously in-

WAKING UP TOO EARLY

The dreams of power(what else now?) break,
and suddenly I lie awake,
and feel the unpolluted joy
and criminal leisure of a boy,
consciously rising for the bait,
the drug, unspied-on hours to wait
here squatting like a dragon on
time's hoard before the day begin.

I cannot take it, I am sick
of stretching for the rhetoric
and hammering allegoric splendor
that forged Goliath's brazen armor,
and shook his Brobdignagian staff
that made the chosen fly like chaff---
so gross the confidence that shone
in meter and iambic line!

Yes, it's more honest to explore
the bottom of the barrel for
its dregs and dreck that seem prfound
because no purpose can be found:
phrases buried in conversation,
headless arrows of imagination,
things forbidden and banished Israel,
because no substance fits the symbol.

Once for a day, or was it weeks,
orr months, I gave up politics,
papers and things that touched the heart,
and lay in a locked room apart,
and adrift and glad to watch a blue
china doorknob, but I could do
nothing to raise it, make it mine,
or bring its meaning into line.

Softer, softer! What if the new
diminuendo brings no true
tenderness, only restlessness,
excess, the hunger for success,
a reckless caution, always first
to fly the field, or find the worst,
running from crisis into crisis---
Prufrock in love with Dionysus!

tended Freudian imagery of phallic power and castration in the poem; and the "Waking Up Too Early" draft seems to me to bear this out. Goliath appears carrying a "Brobdignagian staff" [*sic*]; and when one remembers that he was, ultimately, decapitated, one is interested to see that Lowell refers to his quieter subjects as "headless arrows of imagination" (in the final draft, they become "tools with no handle, / ten candle-ends not worth a candle"). There is little question how orthodox analysis would interpret Lowell's poetic hesitation, in the light of such imagery. The poet fears being castrated if he reveals his full powers and ambitions, literary or ideological; when he prefers subjects without apparent "purpose" or "meaning," he is essentially protecting himself by pretending to be castrated already. This interpretation may help us to understand why Lowell could not, finally, rest content with singing softer, as long as it does not lead us to discount the real dangers—personal and ethical—he saw in breaking loose. The draft ends seemingly still resolved on a "new / diminuendo," but with an unhappy sense that self-contempt will follow the poet whichever direction he chooses: "Prufrock in love with Dionysus!" Beside this, in the margin, a hand, not Lowell's, has firmly written "no!"

The strategy by which Lowell would finally transcend the deadlock in himself shows itself for the first time in one of the first revisions of this rather unfortunate concluding stanza. The last four lines have come to read:

> *Acedia* saved from crime by crisis,
> Prufrock in love with Dionysus,
> shy insolence, and reckless caution,
> soft-spoken, brutal as the nation!

To begin with, Lowell is taking his own restlessness more seriously. It is no longer merely the yearning of any middle-aged Prufrock, but something like the Baudelairean ennui that would "willingly annihilate the earth" (Lowell's translation)—bound to explode outward as "crime" or inward as mental "crisis." Seeing himself so, Lowell sees himself as emblematic: like the nation's, his surface reasonableness is balanced by sudden and extreme outbursts of aggression and brutality. Here the public poem truly begins: analogy will justify the sick poet in passing judgment on his sick country.

In the succeeding drafts, the remaining stanzas file in a few at a time. To judge by a list of rhymes in the margin of "Waking Up Too Early," the stanzas on the Church and its hymns came first, and were intended—like their counterpart, the "dregs and dreck" stanza—as an explicit correlative for one side of Lowell's art: "where Faith, rhyme, meter preach control!" (So Fitzgerald's triad of "excitements religious, political, or poetic" is complete.) Lowell's judgment is essentially negative, but there are telling vacillations: in one draft, there is "no loophole open for the soul" because of Faith, rhyme, and meter; but in another, "dark places crave their stiff control, / and leave a loophole for the soul." (The final version looks like a tidy compromise: "yet they gave darkness some control, / and left a loophole for the soul.") The next stanzas to appear are the third one of the *New York Review* version ("Time to grub up and junk the year's / output"), the opening stanza—initially in third position—and the stanza on "man thinning out his kind"; then comes a preliminary version of the final stanza, then the glass of water.

By the next version I propose to quote in its entirety, "Waking Up (Too) Early On Sunday" (facsimile no. 2), all of the stanzas are present in some form except for the harbor stanza and the stanza about the president; and—allowing for these omissions—the order is as it remained in the *New York Review* version. Gradually, but with visible reluctance, the poem is being rewritten in a more public direction. The stanzas about the Church retain their reference to "rhyme" and "meter," but in the following stanza the poetic "dregs and dreck" have been replaced by the literal objects of the woodshed, with questions of religious and moral—rather than literary—inclusion and exclusion invoked through a series of New Testament allusions. The shifting of the stanza beginning "Oh to break loose" to the first position, and of the one beginning "Sing softer!" away from the last position, indicate a growing acknowledgment that, while a "new / diminuendo" might be desirable, a new crescendo is the emotional fact

WAKING UP(TOO)EARLY ON SUNDAY

Oh to break loose, like the chinook
salmon jumping and falling back,   *NOSING*
horsing up to the impossible
stone and bone-crushing waterfall,
raw-jawed, weak fleshed there, stopped by ten
steps of the roaring ladder, and then
·to clear the top on the last try,
alive enough to spawn and die!

                                                                    VISION
The dreams of power---what else now---break,   *MESSIANIC SACRED*
and suddenly I lie awake,
and feel the unpolluted joy   *body croshpros*
and criminal leisure of a boy---
no rainbow smashing a dry fly   *·*
    in the white run, as free as I,   *IS*
V   here squatting like a dragon on   *know order*
time's hoard before the day begin!

Time to dig up *the year's* and junk the year's   *nescio*
dotage and output of tame verse:
caste-iron whimsy, limp indignation,
liftings, listless self-imitation,
whole days when I could hardly speak,
came barging home unshaven, weak
?   and willing to show anyone   *Read*
/   things done before and better done.

I watch a glass of water wet   *see*
with a fine fuzz of icey sweat,   *∧*
silvery colors touched with sky,
serene in their neutrality---
yet if I shift and change my mood,
I see some object made of wood,
/   background behind it of brown grain,   *fine*
to darken it, but not to stain.

Oh that the spirit could remain
tinged but untarnished by its strain!
Oh better dressed and stacking birch,   *up*
or lost with the Faithful in Church---   *then here in Bob*
∧   Oh anywhere, but somewhere else!   *& NOW*
I hear the new electric bells
clearly chiming, "Faith of our Fathers,"
and now the congregation gathers.

                                                    chopped
Oh Bible mocked and travestied   *Mischen*
by hymns we, h one hears but does not read! *pitoton*
and none of the sweet subtleties   *to sweeter*
of grace or art will gentle these (to)
stiff quatrains shovelled out four-square---
they sing of peace and teach despair---
no loophole open for the soul;
/here Faith, rhyme, reason preach control!
                motor

2.

Throw on old clothes then, and explore
the corners of the woodshed for
its dregs and dreck: tools with no handle,
ten candle-ends not worth a candle,
waste scorned by precept and example,
old lumber banished from the Temple,
cast from the Kingdom, banned in Israel,
the wordless sign, the tinkling cymbal.

Part 3 Christ?

For days now, or is it a week,
I run away from busywork
to lie in my far barn apart,
and when I look into my heart,
I discover none of the great
subjects, death, friendship, love or hate,
I look for doorknobs, marbles, sad,
slight, useless things that calm the mad.

Damned by Paul's precept & example
after for days now on
only our

013

Now on the radio the wars
blare on, earth licks its open sores,
fresh breakage, fresh promotions, chance
assassinations, no advance!
Only man thinning out his kind
sounds through the Sunday noon, the blind
swipe of the pruner and his knife
busy to strip the tree of life.

Now on the television's wars — FLICKERS
about

I cannot take it. One grows sick
of stretching for this rhetoric,
this hammering allegoric splendor,
top-heavy Goliath in full armor
toddling between two hosts, all brass
except its breast-plate, lump and mass,
proped on its brobdignagian staff,
bull-throated bombast stuffed with chaff.

Part for lost splendor

Sing softer! But what if the new
diminuendo brings no true
tenderness, only restlessness,
excess, the hunger for success,
reckless caution fanning its cold
extinct volcano? Only old
Frufrock in love with Dionysus o
picks up the gong and waves the thyrsus.

No, say we fought and trusted in
ourselves to free the earth from sin,
were glad like Ahab to go down
in pride of righteousness, and drown,
that we were faithful to this boast,
our appetite for which we lost the
the world, though free of other crime,
in the monotonous sublime.

say
Guilty

For this, & for no other crime
Guiltless of any other crime, we perish lost our earth & ghost
Forever & forever lost
In the monotonous sublime.

behind the poem. The great stanza on the Vietnam War is now in almost final form (though without Johnson it requires an introductory reference to "the radio" or "the television," so that the verb "flicker" actually enters the poem referring to the TV screen, and not to the fires of napalm). But even this stanza stirs up Lowell's uneasiness about grandeur and indignation, for in the following Goliath stanza he now specifies, "One grows sick / of stretching for *this* rhetoric" (italics mine).

But it is the last three stanzas that are still the farthest from their final form, and thereby perhaps the most indicative of what remains unresolved in the direction of the poem. For reasons which will become evident, I intend to discuss the first of the three, the Goliath stanza, last. In the "Sing softer" stanza we see, once again, the initially personal reference of a metaphor later externalized—the "cold / extinct volcano," later "the planet" itself—is here Lowell's own quickly exhausted or suppressed access of energy. The Prufrock reference now seems to be coupled with another allusion, to the scene in Euripides' *The Bacchae* where Cadmus and Teiresias go out, thyrsus in hand, "to forget . . . old age" dancing among the followers of Dionysus. When one remembers that King Pentheus—the figure of military puritanism who mocks their easy conversion—ends up torn to pieces for his impiety, the comparison becomes less unflattering to Lowell than first appears. (As is, I hope, obvious, the thyrsus as a phallic symbol duplicates Goliath's "Brobdignagian staff"—also a property of Lowell's engaged self—and contrasts with the "candle-ends" and "doorknobs" of his quieter mode.)

So it may not be altogether surprising that the last stanza begins with what seems, at first glance, a long overdue reversal of feeling: suppose Lowell did, after all this conscience-searching, trust himself enough to fight wholeheartedly for his notion of justice? But this resolve darkens into fatalism almost as quickly as the impulse to "break loose" does in the opening stanza. The reference to Ahab is a poetic reworking of prose statements in two interviews with A. Alvarez. In the first (*London Observer*, 21 July 1963), Lowell said:

if I have an image of it [America], it would be one taken from Melville's *Moby Dick:* the fanatical idealist who brings the world down in ruins through some sort of simplicity of mind. I believe that's in our character and in my own personal character; I reflect that it's a danger for us.

In the later interview (*Encounter* 24, February 1965), he elaborated:

We were founded on a Declaration, on the Constitution, on Principles, and we've always had the ideal of "saving the world." And that comes close to perhaps destroying the world. . . . We might blow up Cuba to save ourselves and then the whole world would blow up. Yet it would come in the guise of an idealistic stroke. . . . it is the Ahab story of having to murder evil: and you may murder all the good with it if it gets desperate enough to struggle.

But Lowell went on to say that "what's best in our country in a way is united with this. . . . a kind of energy and power of imagination of throwing yourself all out into something." Elsewhere in the interview, he applied to the national temperament the three adjectives "biblical," "Jewish," and "Messianic"—all telling for "Waking Early" (in some drafts the salmon is called a "Messianic vision").

The interviews make clear, I think, that we have partially misread the stanza; that when Lowell speaks of a "we" bent on freeing "the earth from sin," he means both "our character and . . . my own personal character": both his own liberal crusading impulse and the national anticommunism—rooted in the Puritan sense of absolute good and evil—that makes the Vietnam War almost self-ratifying, whatever its pragmatic value. There is, it would seem, less difference than first appears between the martyr's willingness to lose the world and the superpower's calculated risk of destroying it.[2] Lowell is, again, deliberately conflating his own faults with those of his adversaries, to the point of an almost total ambiguity of reference. In this context, the phrase "monotonous sublime" is freighted mainly with a literary and ethical critique of idealism, not the Pascalian metaphysical emptiness that makes the final version so memorable.

Still, Lowell has, in fact, allowed a good deal of public and ethical judgment to enter the poem since the "Waking Up Too Early" draft. But as he has given himself this freedom, his Goliath has—like the picture of Dorian Gray—grown ever more hollow and deliquescent. Now "propped" on his staff rather than shaking it, padded "with chaff" to fill his over-sized armor (or "bombast"), he "toddles" in childlike senility "between two hosts"—as Lowell may have felt uneasily sand-wiched between the ruling elite of his own generation and the intolerant, Dionysiac young who shared his immediate poli-tics. Clearly, the inward crisis of conscience has deepened rather than resolved itself.

At the same time, Lowell seems subtly aware that Goliath makes an incongruous comparison for so moral, even "Messi-anic," a warrior as himself. The only overt reference—imme-diately discarded—to his own political act in the manuscripts speaks of "the Jews, who seldom dined / with the opposition." (Perhaps it is not too fanciful to think this line led Lowell, associatively, to an occasion when the Jews did offer to mingle with "the opposition," then smote them, as Dionysus smote Pentheus, in their virility: the circumcision and slaughter of the Shechemites, "a million foreskins stacked like trash.") And one cannot help remembering Lowell's earlier use of David, the idealist "tyrannicide," and Goliath in "Florence"—which he in fact echoes, rather sardonically, on the same manuscript page where the reference to the Jews appears: "Pity the mon-ster, but why refuse / this gallant foeman we can use?"

The "use" of the "foeman," when it comes, comes with staggering rapidity. In the next version, anticipated in the margin of "Waking Up (Too) Early On Sunday," we read:

> Pray for lost statesmen. One grows sick
> of stretching for their rhetoric,
> and coarse apocalyptic clamor:
> top-heavy Goliath in full armor

and then, in the next one, this:

> Pray for a statesman. One grows sick
> of the ghost-written rhetoric,
> the coarse apocalyptic clamor,
> top-heavy Johnson in full armor.

The equation of Lowell's worst vision of himself with Johnson acts like a chemical catalyst on the poem. Everything explodes and resettles. On the very next page of the drafts, the Johnson stanza appears—except for two words—in its final form. The Goliath material, when it next appears, is appropriately applied to American militarism, not to writing; and the mistrust of high-style poetry has—except for the brief injunction to "Sing softer"—vanished from the poem, entirely translated into its political and religious counterterms. One might say— to relish the matter in its full circularity—that Lowell can now write with a clear conscience about the bad public world because that world *is* the bad self that wants to write about it. (Even the disagreeable fact that people want Lowell to write public poems has its parallel, in a quickly canceled passage wishing "Peace / to presidents condemned to horse / the universe in line by force.") But the real marvel is that, within the space of one page, Lowell's identification with Johnson has deepened to include not only their delinquescent overextensions of themselves but the most primordially human and valuable level of their explosive energies:

> Oh to break loose now. All life's grandeur
> is something with a girl in summer.

In redeeming his own energetic self, Lowell has, willy-nilly, redeemed Johnson's as well.

Here we have, essentially, arrived at the *New York Review* version. But I would like to pause, at this point, over some slight late revisions which reveal less about thematic development than they do about the nature of genius. As the poem has gotten more traditionally grand in its total ambitions, it has gotten more and not less daring in its use of low-style vocabularies—slang, advertising, political journalese—and of shrill, discordant tones. The last marginal revisions of the

Goliath stanza are a case in point. The typed version to which they are appended reads:

> This hammering military splendor,
> top-heavy Goliath in full armor,
> little to please us in the mass
> maneuvers of Philistine brass,
> tactics and ballistics moving
> with the times and still improving,
> when their kingdom cracked in half,
> and vanished like a pile of chaff.

In all cases, it is the quieter, more neutral expressions that are replaced—by slangy journalese ("hit the crash," "liquidations of their brass"), religious hyperbole ("redemption" for "to please us"), an archaic specification ("elephant and phalanx" for "tactics and ballistics") which heightens, by contrast, the adman's language that follows ("moving / with the times and still improving"). The most drastic substitution of all ("a million foreskins stacked like trash") shoves forward, with bold free-associative abruptness, the sexual preoccupations in the poem, in particular the subliminal concern with castration. But the biblical allusion also, as I have suggested elsewhere, adds to the moral complexity of the poem; it lessens the gap between the behavior of the Jews—Lowell's prototype for the "Messianic" side of himself, and of America—and that of their "monster" adversaries.

Instances could be multiplied in which an increase in stridency simultaneously enriches the meaning of the poem. There is the late introduction of drug slang ("fixed and kicked") into the "Sing softer" stanza. There is the replacement of "Oh Bible mocked and travestied" by "Oh Bible chopped and crucified"—a histrionic, even hysterical, sounding phrase which, for the careful reader, joins the Bible, in its fuller, untidier meanings, to the "brown grain" of experience, the "old lumber banished from the Temple," and the "tree of life" itself, all roughly handled by the impulse to idealistic simplification.

What does vanish from the poem, on the other hand, is a

kind of self-conscious, apologetic irony, the author guarding a certain neutral distance from his own excesses. We hear no more of "Prufrock in love with Dionysus." Instead of passing his own wry, literary critic's judgment on his abortive poems— "cast-iron whimsy, limp indignation"—Lowell now takes the riskier tack of using the labels his work receives and, at its worst, courts, from second-rate literary journalism: "dim confession, coy revelation." There is, thus, a constant convergence of the speaking voice in the poem both with the hyperbolic, restless self described—"fixed and kicked by reckless caution"—and with the overexcited mass consciousness, mass language, of which that self has become emblematic. A lesser poet would have been afraid thus to depart from correct, defensible statement, in a poem of public truths; we see here the peculiar combination of self-trust and surrender to the subject matter which so often separates genius from talent.

For many readers, the *New York Review* version of the poem represented the ideal balance between personal and public content, from which all departure was deterioration. The limited amount of literary self-portraiture Lowell had left in the poem—the poet pushing his second-best work on his friends or, indeed, "anyone"; or trying, without success, to reach his own feelings about "the great / subjects: death, friendship, love and hate"—seemed, in several important ways, to authenticate the poem. They made Lowell's humility, in this increasingly "Biblical" work, specific, and therefore more real; they gave the evidence for Lowell's claim that he, in some way, resembled Lyndon Johnson; and they made the paradoxical drama of arriving at "the great subjects" through an examination of incapacities take place, visibly, in the poem itself. But clearly, for Lowell himself, the process of analogical substitution, by which the poem had turned outward, and away from the personal, was more easily started than stopped. And so— in the same way that the Church and the woodshed stanzas had been rewritten earlier—Lowell's numbness before the "great subjects" found its equivalent in our collective reliance on symbols of transcendence (the "old spire and flag- / pole") that had become as disconnected as the madman's doorknob. When Lowell also eliminated the stanza about his own "dry verse," he gave the underlying sense of lacking an adequate outlet for his new energy its objective correlative: the "creatures of the night" seeking for "unstopped holes" at daybreak, or mindlessly rolling "a marble, hours on end." (The "marble" had appeared in an earlier draft coupled with the china doorknob. An excised simile once made the allegory of self-entrapment explicit: "a chipmunk rolls / a marble somewhere, as the mind gnaws / into the clockwork of its laws.")

The arrangement of the final stanzas had, as the drafts make clear, troubled Lowell even before the magazine version. (There, the order is Johnson—Vietnam—Goliath—"Sing softer"—"Pity the planet"; in the book it becomes Goliath—"Sing softer"—Johnson—Vietnam—"Pity the planet.") I think one can at least guess at the conflicting considerations in Lowell's mind. It was clearly unsatisfactory to have the Johnson stanza—both more of a tour de force, and more central, than the Goliath stanza—in an earlier and less climactic position. Before the magazine version, Lowell had toyed with placing it next to last, between "Sing softer" and "Pity the planet," but had rejected this, perhaps because it seemed unnatural to separate the Johnson stanza from the Vietnam stanza. On the other hand, the other two stanzas also, in a sense, formed a bloc. Lowell would no longer have wished, as in the "Waking Up (Too) Early On Sunday" draft, to attach any disclaimer to the rhetoric of the Vietnam stanza; the injunction to "Sing softer" found its appropriate occasion in the calculated eruption of the primitive psychological side of ideological struggle at the end of the Goliath stanza. Lowell's ultimate decision was simply to reverse the two blocs of stanzas. But one consequence of this arrangement, whether intended or not, was to make a "new / diminuendo" ever less part of the final tonal effect of the poem; shoved three stanzas back, it became a nostalgic last glance toward some pastoral world where energy exhausted itself as "something with a girl in summer." Lowell's private turmoil was banished from the concluding movement of the poem, which now widened with impersonal and public logic, and with increasing prophetic grandeur, from Johnson to his war to the future of "the planet" itself.

Whether Lowell in the end, ironically, made "Waking Early" too public a poem—"cold" and "dutiful," as one particularly harsh critic put it—cannot be settled here.[3] I hope I have suggested how difficult it would have been for Lowell to make the clearly valuable changes after the magazine version without also making the more questionable ones. (The Johnson stanza could easily follow the original china doorknobs stanza; but could the Goliath stanza, without the intrusion of the phallic-patriotic "spire and flag- / pole"?) But it is more important to remember that the late changes are, at worst, overextensions of a principle—the analogical substitution of public for private material—which accounts for the entire growth of the poem. This principle reflects, in miniature, the grand structure of Lowell's best work from "Memories of West Street and Lepke" through *History;* and by virtue of it, a poem initially about as interesting as earlier poems of total self-blockage like "Eye and Tooth" became the one great poem to emerge from the protest movement against the Vietnam War.

It would be surprising if, in a poem so exhaustively revised, we had not lost very good writing as well as been spared poor. I should like to conclude by quoting the one truly beautiful stanza which vanished without a trace. It appears to have been written at the same time as the "creatures of the night" stanza, to extend the literal description of early morning which Lowell then, presumably, decided already took up ample room. But it also serves to clarify one of the poem's sadder themes, that the "good works," the self-sufficing energies, tapped in sleep are misshapen by the limited applications daylight and critical consciousness allow:

> Some door's unbolted, loosened boards
> murmur, then a thousand roused birds
> shake the deceptive daybreak storm
> with their tense half-hour alarm;
> my papery window shades begin
> to tremble under their thin tan,
> they blaze like shavings. Too much light!
> The good works of the night give out.

Notes

1. The drafts of "Waking Early Sunday Morning" are housed in the Houghton Library, bMS Am 1905 (2337), and are quoted by permission of the Houghton Library, Harvard University, and of the Estate of Robert Lowell.

2. Two echoes in this stanza seem to reinforce a theme implicit throughout—the sexual basis of political self-intoxication. In Lowell's translation of Canto XV of the *Inferno*, Brunetto Latini speaks of "the world / we soiled and lost for our one common crime" (homosexuality). A marginal variant in the draft includes the phrase "the world well lost"—the subtitle of Dryden's play about Antony and Cleopatra.

3. I have chosen not to discuss the further revisions contained in *Selected Poems*, since Lowell himself thought better of them before the paperback edition of that book.

A Cold Spring
Elizabeth Bishop as Poet of Feeling

I

"Those who restrain desire, do so because theirs is weak enough to be restrained," William Blake wrote; but the same is not necessarily true of poets who handle feeling obliquely. It is increasingly evident that the force of Elizabeth Bishop's poetry is not altogether accounted for by that image of her so often put forward, in praise or blame: the heiress apparent of Marianne Moore; the crowning glory of a canon of taste that emphasized surface exactitude, the elimination of the personal, and an arch, slightly inhibiting, self-consciousness about how the imagination works. I should therefore like to focus attention on Bishop's one sustained attempt at a passionately personal kind of lyric: the seemingly little read, little discussed love poems of *A Cold Spring*. The very strangeness—and, occasionally, the failure—of these poems has much to teach us, not only about Bishop's reasons for reticence, but about the vision of life, the aura or underfeeling, that subtly animates her more reticent poetry (a poetry which also, paradoxically or not so paradoxically, assumed its most persistent shape, the travel narrative, in this same second volume).

My basic contention is that, if Bishop characteristically distanced emotion, it was partly because emotion for her—and especially feelings of despair, loneliness, apprehension—ten-

From *Elizabeth Bishop and Her Art,* ed. Lloyd Schwartz and Sybil P. Estess (Ann Arbor: University of Michigan Press, 1983).

ded to become immense and categorical, insusceptible to rational or, in poetry, to structural counterargument. There is a curious disproportion to many of the love poems in *A Cold Spring*, created by the tyrannical assertiveness, the refusal to engage in dialogue, of the darker feelings; and especially by a kind of ground-conviction that reciprocal love is, almost metaphysically, impossible. Consider the conclusion of "Insomnia":

> So wrap up care in a cobweb
> and drop it down the well
>
> into that world inverted
> where left is always right,
> where the shadows are really the body,
> where we stay awake all night,
> where the heavens are shallow as the sea
> is now deep, and you love me.

The last line admits of two readings, neither very cheery: that you "now" love me (but how deep is the sea, when compared with the heavens?); or that the phrase "you love me" is one of a series of impossible propositions, conceivable only in the narcissist's mirror world "where left is always right." But from the reader's point of view, what is most shocking about this grim assessment is the way one is led to it without the least hint that a "you" is at issue in the poem; and then—as if the subject were too painful to bear more than the briefest mention—suddenly dropped. The naked emotion of the ending is pointed up by the contrasting tone of jaunty insouciance, pretend optimism, with which the sentence begins.

Such an effect verges on melodramatic indulgence; for me, the line is crossed in "Varick Street." There, the disproportion lies in the juxtaposition of the three purely descriptive stanzas, presenting the neighborhood where "Our bed / shrinks from the soot," with the thrice-repeated refrain:

> *And I shall sell you sell you*
> *sell you of course, my dear, and you'll sell me.*

Why?—the irritable voice of reason might ask—simply because they live on an ugly industrial street? The inner eye, casting back through the poem, might reply that the factories amount, from the beginning, to a nightmare image of the human body and its imperfections—

> wretched uneasy buildings
> veined with pipes
> attempt their work.
> Trying to breathe,
> the elongated nostrils
> haired with spikes
> give off such stenches, too

—and that the definition of "certain wonders"—

> Pale dirty light,
> some captured iceberg
> being prevented from melting

—suggests that the wonderful is something frigid, remote, self-sufficient (as in "The Imaginary Iceberg"), unnaturally half-preserved in the "dirty" glare and heat of physical contact. But such readings are strained and emblem-bookish, while the crying voice is commonplace, reasonless, shrill; a middle ground of normal human judgment cannot be established, and the poem fails to jell. One feels, as in "Insomnia," that the poet has been swept away by a monolithic, unarguable intuition of implacable fate.

Bishop was never guilty of such imbalances again; yet even *Geography III*—justly praised for its calm and direct treatment of personal themes—is ghosted with the same abruptness in the face of painful feeling. The jauntiness which insists on representing defeat as triumph (and which is not self-deception, rather a peculiar exercise of pride: Anne Winters has compared it to the smile in the voice of a blues singer) is the basic premise of "One Art." The trick of turning the poem to an overwhelming personal sorrow in the last line—and then turning it off—reappears in "Five Flights Up," though here, perhaps wisely, only the force, and not the cause, of the sorrow is given:

> —Yesterday brought to today so lightly!
> (A yesterday I find almost impossible to lift.)

("One Art," too, waits till the last stanza to tell the reader that a lover's specific anxiety lies behind its general concern with "The art of losing.")

The love poems in *A Cold Spring* betray an immense anxiety about the adjustments between inner and outer worlds. The narcissistic emphasis of "Insomnia," the disbelief in reciprocal love, is one mode of this anxiety; a difficulty in distinguishing feeling from judgment is another. So far, we have been aware of the latter mainly negatively, as a weakness in the poems. Some poems, however, manage to make the confusion itself part of their manifest content. A playful, almost medieval, allegory underlines the speaker's inability to see the "Days and Distance" of a separation as neutral facts, and not as a malign "Argument" against love. Elsewhere, love itself is defined as the state in which "a name / and all its connotation are the same."

The happiest poem, personally and artistically, of the whole group is one involving both an interchange between people, and an interchange between feelings and realities, "Rain towards Morning" (quoted here in its entirety):

> The great light cage has broken up in the air,
> freeing, I think, about a million birds
> whose wild ascending shadows will not be back,
> and all the wires come falling down.
> No cage, no frightening birds; the rain
> is brightening now. The face is pale
> that tried the puzzle of their prison
> and solved it with an unexpected kiss,
> whose freckled unsuspected hands alit.

All of the imagistic terms of this strange aubade have both an inner and an outer meaning. The "great light cage" of rain is also an intrapsychic cage, as the punning description already suggests: it is both substantial, a "cage" imprisoning "light"—as a "bear cage" imprisons bears—and insubstantial, gone in an instant, a "light cage." The literal birds soaring at dawn call up associations of romantic—basically orgasmic—release that go back, in poetry, at least as far as Bernard de Ventadour. But when the birds are seen as caged—as repressed impulses inside the psyche—they are suddenly reseen as "frightening," the devouring birds or harpies of nightmare. Finally, the birds are tamed by being externalized once more, but not to as great a distance: they become the tremulous, frightened motions of the "unexpected," "unsuspected" lovers themselves, suddenly alighting on each other. The very fact that inward and outward things can be brought as close together as such imagery suggests; that an action, or another person, can "solve" an intrapsychic "puzzle," is greeted, in the poem, with a combination of joy, astonishment, and fear. "The face is pale" as after a struggle or a shattering revelation. And though the world is, indeed, lit up ("alit" has this punning double sense, I think), the old fear that love is evanescent, that dependence is already loss, can still be felt. It is there in the very image of birds finding a temporary perch; and in the seemingly inappropriate elegiac feeling about release itself— "will not be back." An impersonal despair is still very near the surface. But bounds have been set to it; the psychological nature of the impasse is partly acknowledged; and the result is at least one great, or near-great, poem of personal love.

II

For a poet so obsessed with the distance between human beings—and inclined to see the connections as illusory, muddling, transitory at best—the tourist's-eye view of life is not only comfortingly manageable but, in a fundamental way, *correct*. For the traveler, other people are necessarily remote, unknowable, almost interchangeable; the first flicker of attraction or interest toward an individual is already elegy. The multiplication in space of people doing almost the same things almost simultaneously—but utterly unknown to each other— has some of the annihilating effect of the multiplication in time, in a foreshortening of the centuries. The traveler, like Chaucer, knows that the earth is not home, but wilderness.

"Cape Breton" achieves such a vision simply by moving slowly across a landscape where all activities have been interrupted by an old-fashioned Sunday. From these interruptions is extrapolated a feeling of arbitrariness, of absurd or mysterious purposelessness, about almost anything being exactly where and as it is. The churches "have been dropped into the matted hills / like lost quartz arrowheads"; the road, like the bulldozers, looks "abandoned." On the cliffs "the silly-looking puffins all stand . . . in solemn uneven lines"; while sheep, frightened by the noise of airplanes, actually stampede into the sea and kill themselves. Even the sheen of the water seems to be "weaving and weaving" a Penelope's web, that disappears "under the mist equally in all directions." The one appealing human figure in the poem, a man carrying a baby, removes himself toward an "invisible house," through a meadow which, in a wonderful oxymoron, "establishes its poverty in a snowfall of daisies." Half-playfully explicit about its own effect, the poem suggests that

> Whatever the landscape had of meaning appears to have
> been abandoned,
> unless the road is holding it back, in the interior,
> where we cannot see

But all we find in the interior is

> miles of burnt forests standing in gray scratches
> like the admirable scriptures made on stones by stones—

a vision of elaboration without intention almost as subversive of "scripture" itself as of the homiletic-pastoral of Shakespeare's "sermons in stones."

The same distrust of human readings of nature fills the title poem, "A Cold Spring"—a poem which also deserves our attention as a kind of (again, structurally) troubling middle ground between the poems of touristic detachment and the personal lyrics. It is basically a happy poem; but few happy poems are simultaneously so skeptical about the reasonless metonymies of happiness we are willing to accept. (Only the great opening section of Eugenio Montale's "Times at Bellosguardo" comes to mind.) Bishop begins by quoting Hopkins—"Nothing is so beautiful as spring"—but her uneasiness about the automatic affirmativeness of the season is quickly projected onto almost the entire natural order. "The trees hesitated," though "carefully indicating their characteristics"; "the violet was flawed on the lawn"; a newborn calf seems "inclined to feel gay," but its mother, eating the "wretched" afterbirth, quite clearly does not. There is a feeling—even as the weather finally warms up—of something mechanical, contrived about the whole process:

> Song-sparrows were wound up for the summer,
> and in the maple the complimentary cardinal
> cracked a whip

Then the poem moves into the present tense and, rather wonderfully, relaxes, yields:

> Now, in the evening,
> a new moon comes.
> The hills grow softer. Tufts of long grass show
> where each cow-flop lies.
> The bull-frogs are sounding,
> slack strings plucked by heavy thumbs.

The concentration of long and short *o*s and *u*s makes the passage itself sound rather like a cello solo—slow, darkened, languorous. At the same time, there is just enough dissonance in the content to maintain a sense of limit, of uncertain grounding. The grass grows longer over cow-flops; the "bull-frogs" sound like "slack strings"; the fireflies rise only so high and no higher, "exactly like the bubbles in champagne." Yet the poem qualifies, "Later on they rise much higher"—thus leaving the growth of its own exhilaration, by implication, equally uncurtailed.

"A Cold Spring" becomes a problematic poem because of a teasingly absent-present further dimension: the question being whether, as so often in literature, the yielding to spring is itself a metonymy for the yielding to love. The word "your" occurs four times in the poem—always as an ascription of property, but, still, often enough to call attention to itself. The first and last appearances of the word—"your big and aimless hills," "your shadowy pastures"—easily suggest an eroticized fusion of landscape and body. Perhaps the velleitous, unresolved state of these hints has something to do with the curiously anticlimactic tone of the last three lines of the poem:

> And your shadowy pastures will be able to offer
> these particular glowing tributes
> every evening now throughout the summer.

The next-to-last line—redolent of the most formal occasions of congratulation, after-dinner speeches, blurbs—for a long time seemed to me a mere embarrassed stiffening at having to express joy, as wrong, and as telltale, as the abruptnesses of "Varick Street" or "Insomnia." Now, however, it occurs to me that Bishop may have intended such an effect, from the moment she brought in the "champagne"; that she perhaps wished the reader to feel that something over-formal, and a little sad, occurs whenever we stand back and try to ratify how much "higher" we have risen or can rise—in a season, in our powers of feeling, or in love. The line between a defensive archness and a philosophically expressive one is peculiarly hard to draw here; for that very reason, we are left more sharply aware of the dangers Bishop faced, and of the nature of her success, in her more impersonal work.

The just balance between surface archness and detachment and subliminal emotional intensity is finally struck—as it will be again and again in the best of Bishop's later work—in "At the Fishhouses" and "Over 2000 Illustrations and a Complete Concordance." At the center of the latter (since I do not have space to discuss both poems in detail) is a vision of desolate accumulation comparable to that in "Cape Breton"— though this judgment will seem paradoxical as soon as I start to quote:

> And at St. Peter's the wind blew and the sun shone madly.
> Rapidly, purposefully, the Collegians marched in lines,
> crisscrossing the great square with black, like ants.
> In Mexico the dead man lay
> in a blue arcade; the dead volcanoes
> glistened like Easter lilies.

The jukebox went on playing "Ay, Jalisco!"
And at Volubilis there were beautiful poppies
splitting the mosaics; the fat old guide made eyes.
In Dingle harbor a golden length of evening
the rotting hulks held up their dripping plush.
The Englishwoman poured tea, informing us
that the Duchess was going to have a baby.
And in the brothels of Marrakesh
the little pockmarked prostitutes
balanced their tea-trays on their heads
and did their belly-dances; flung themselves
naked and giggling against our knees,
asking for cigarettes.

Desolate?—the reader may well ask. Surely, taken piece by piece—and in the brilliance of its modulations—this is one of the best, and most exuberant, poetic catalogs since Whitman. The careful contraction toward, and expansion away from, the minimal two-line unit; the hurrying, irregular, long-breathed march of the Collegians, marshaled along by their adverbs, set against the andante of Mexico; the "golden length of evening" which seems outside of time because it is spatial as well, the "length" of the moss-gilded hulks themselves . . . one could go on enumerating beauties indefinitely. And yet there is a terrible, and a touristic, detachment about this passage which is finally most un-Whitmanesque. The "dead man," so carefully paired with the beautiful "dead volcanoes," and given appropriate mood music, becomes, inevitably, one frisson among many; the world in which the duchess's baby is respectable before birth is blankly, without commentary, the same world in which some children are virtually born prostitutes. The world is everything that is the case; or, as Bishop puts it a few lines later, "Everything only connected by 'and' and 'and.'"

What saves this catalog from a final coldness may be the slight "confessional" shock of the brothel scene. Because this is something one does not see without a choice, a choice that might arouse shame, and certainly rouses the reader's curiosity—yes, Miss Bishop went places she could not have taken Miss Moore, any more than Hart Crane could take his grandmother!—the speaker is suddenly, and vulnerably, part of the spectacle. Thus we are prepared for the more intimate, introspective voice that addresses us immediately thereafter: "It was somewhere near there / I saw what frightened me most of all."

What frightens the speaker is, in fact, a peculiarly striking emblem of the disintegration of vulnerable individuals into mere spectacle, mere phenomenon: "A holy grave, not looking particularly holy . . . open to every wind from the pink desert" and "half-filled with dust, not even the dust / of the poor prophet paynim who once lay there." That this unprotecting grave is "carved solid / with exhortation"—presumably from the Koran—is a further proof of human impotence, but also, of course, a critique *en abime* of the poem's own too solid effort to cover and preserve everything.

But the poem does not end on this vision of meaningless-ness. In "our travels," we have, it goes without saying, failed to see the one thing that might really have mattered. (In the prototype of all voyage poems, Baudelaire observed that no real foreign city quite measures up to *ceux que le hasard fait avec les nuages*.) For what is truly satisfying, we must return to the child's book where our desire to travel had its start:

> Open the heavy book. Why couldn't we have seen
> this old Nativity while we were at it?
> —the dark ajar, the rocks breaking with light,
> an undisturbed, unbreathing flame,
> colorless, sparkless, freely fed on straw,
> and, lulled within, a family with pets,
> —and looked and looked our infant sight away.

"The dark ajar" is, in its largest reverberations, an image of mystical revelation—"breaking" through the rocklife surface of phenomena to their permanent, essential being, sheltered in the "unbreathing flame" of eternal Mind. But it also sug-gests a poignant little story, of a stranger (or perhaps a child who has been sent to bed) peering in at the brightness of the family circle—the opposite of that final solitude which the brothel and the grave, in their different ways, represent. And it is, I think, from the tension between these poles of human and emotional, as well as ontological, experience that the poem gathers its seriousness and force. David Kalstone has suggested how relevant Elizabeth Bishop's own experience of an essentially parentless childhood is here. And that relevance extends, surely, to many of the issues we have been concerned with throughout: the easy assumption of an uninvolved, spectator's stance toward life; the a priori pessimism about intimate relationships; the potentially monolithic despair. This is not the place to develop the biographical side of Kalstone's insight, since it is the literary consequences of this complex of attitudes that concern us here. But we might note that Bishop's last great voyage poem, "The Moose," follows the same trajectory as "Over 2000 Illustrations," from the traveler's atomized world back to a scene of familial enclosure, overheard by a half-included, half-isolated child. (The specification, there, of "grandparents" rather than parents makes the child, more clearly than ever, Bishop herself.)

I have confined myself to *A Cold Spring* because, containing as it does such opposite kinds of poems, it seems to bring to a focus the problem of feeling in Bishop's work; and not because it seems to me (apart from "Over 2000 Illustrations" and "At the Fishhouses") her highest achievement as a poet. That distinction would have to go either to her first book, *North & South* (in which feeling keeps its intensity by a projection at times almost as visionary as Hart Crane's); or to her last, *Geography III* (in which feeling is meditated on, grandly, plainly, and in relative tranquility, after being very slightly universalized). Let me then, in conclusion—and in lieu of the psychological speculations I have curtailed—turn back to one of the early visionary poems for Bishop's own portrait of herself as a rather special case of the poet of feeling.

In that fey creature, "The Man-Moth," are condensed several more and less familiar myths of the artist. He is *Pierrot lunaire,* the lover of the moon, of unattainable ideals and romantic strangeness; though this is a role he shares, a little, with mere ordinary Man, blindly "magnetized to the moon." On a more refined level, he suggests the Keatsian image of the artist without personality, reducible to "a photographer's cloak" and a camera eye. But finally and most importantly, he is the person who cannot take the outer world for granted, but must see it at the drastic extremes of process—a struggle to be born, or a menace of dying. Believing the moon to be "a small hole at the top of the sky, / proving the sky quite useless for protection," he tries, though it is "what [he] fears most,"

> to push his small head through that round clean opening
> and be forced through, as from a tube, in black scrolls
>   on the light.

(The image combines absorption into the external, photography, with self-expression, writing or painting—as it combines annihilation and birth.)

Further on, we find other metaphors for this inability to proportion the world to oneself. Motion (including, implicitly, the motion of time) becomes a nauseating vertigo: in the subway,

> The Man-Moth always seats himself facing the wrong way
> and the train starts at once at its full, terrible speed,
> without a shift in gears or a gradation of any sort.
> He cannot tell the rate at which he travels backwards.

Both actual life and the life of the psyche present themselves as a smooth, seamless, entrapping superficies ("artificial tunnels and . . . recurrent dreams"). Yet one absolute is ever-present: "the third rail, the unbroken draught of posion," which "he regards . . . as a disease / he has inherited the susceptibility to." Here, one can hardly help thinking of some of Bishop's later choices as a poet—her seamless, apparently depthless, cataloging ("Everything only connected by 'and' and 'and' "), combined with the constant undercurrent of intimations of mortality.

Yet "The Man-Moth" ends with an extraordinarily charged and traumatic image for the expression of the inner self. As the Man-Moth, earlier, expected to be squeezed through the hole in the sky, so "one tear . . . slips" from his eye—"an entire night itself"—when a flashlight is held up to it. This tear is, in his orphaned perception, "his only possession," and, "like the bee's sting," presumably death to lose. The image can, I think, stand as our final emblem both for the peculiarly beleaguered mode of introversion or narcissism in Bishop's character, and for the way in which her feelingful self did—never without some sense of trauma—enter the world in her poems. Bishop warns us that the Man-Moth will protect himself if he can: "Slyly he palms it [the tear]"

> and if you're not paying attention
> he'll swallow it. However, if you watch, he'll hand
> it over,
> cool as from underground springs and pure enough to drink.

Bishop did, in fact, sometimes "palm" the emotional dimension of her poems almost too successfully. But for those who knew how to pay attention, it was always there—an ambiance, a *lacrimae rerum,* which, even as it presented a "pure," "cool" transparency toward things as they are, testified to the "underground" emotional personality of its creator.

A Poetry of Limits
Philip Larkin (1922–1985)

> Strange to know nothing, never to be sure
> Of what is true or right or real,
> But forced to qualify *or so I feel,*
> Or *Well, it does seem so:*
> *Someone must know.*

The voice is unmistakable: intimate without being personal,
like Rilke's; eloquent without ever avoiding the common-
place; always a little rueful, defeatist, or at least resigned.
Some readers are a little troubled at being so intimately in-
cluded in the resignation. They would rather see it as a British
national weakness; or as the private fear of life of a provincial
librarian who never married, never traveled farther than Ire-
land, and is said to have refused the poet laureateship because
he was convinced he would never write again. Yet the voice of
"Ignorance," the poem I began by quoting, is not unaware of
what stands against resignation—everything from biological
programming to sexual need to the possibility of psychologi-
cal change, all implied in the next stanza's wonderfully slip-
pery, categorical generalities:

> Strange to be ignorant of the way things work:
> Their skill at finding what they need,
> Their sense of shape, and punctual spread of seed,
> And willingness to change

Threepenny Review 8, no. 2 (summer 1987).

The poem ends holding both visions in a kind of double focus:

> Yes, it is strange
>
> Even to wear such knowledge—for our flesh
> Surrounds us with its own decisions—
> And yet spend all our life on imprecisions,
> That when we start to die
> Have no idea why.

The last lines require a characteristic double take. It is our "imprecisions" that "Have no idea why" we die, as they have no idea why we live as we do; *we* know perfectly well, yet are condemned to "spend all our life" on the level of imprecision, the deeper knowledge being forever unsearchable to our conscious minds.

If these limits to hope and certainty seem in some way ultimate ones, which we can imagine escaping, but never really escape for long, then perhaps it is time, in the months following his death, to reconsider our image of Philip Larkin as a narrow, over-rational, self-deprecating pessimist. For that image simply overlooks too much, not only in the way of philosophical seriousness but of sensuous beauty, compassion, and empathy, an erotic feeling or, more largely, a "thinking of the body" which his life predisposes us not to look for in him. Finally, it overlooks the purely stylistic largeness of a poet who not only combines the high lyrical and the demotic more successfully than any poet in English since Frost, but has a surrealist high frequency which is, again, the last thing we are accustomed to expect from him. To see how elemental—not British, not provincial, hardly socially voiced at all—Larkin's style can become, and at the same time to catch this surrealist register, consider another short poem from *The Whitsun Weddings,* "Days":

> What are days for?
> They come, they wake us
> Time and time over.
> They are to be happy in:
> Where can we live but days?

> Ah, solving that question
> Brings the priest and the doctor
> In their long coats
> Running over the fields.

In an odd way, Blake's *Songs of Innocence* seem the nearest precedent for this disillusioned poem, with its mixture of nursery-rhyme tautological simplicity and fantasy. The last lines are, of course, a clever way of saying that we "solve that question" only by dying. But they also inevitably include the intellectual enterprises by which "the priest and the doctor" have tried to figure out a way to live outside of space and time—and so escape contingency, escape fragmentation. And they are magical lines because of the surreal, absurd, Edenic costume and garden party to which they reduce (or elevate) these solemn undertakings. That is where the Blakean Innocence comes in, in spite of the poem's skeptical melancholy.

The best of Larkin's poems combine this magical quality not only with "the still, sad music of humanity," but with an expansive identification, fleshly as well as spiritual, which is more like Whitman than Wordsworth. My very favorite poem of this kind is "The Whitsun Weddings." It is about a train trip from Hull to London, and it begins with two stanzas of brilliant, slow, almost haphazard landscape description—

> All windows down, all cushions hot, all sense
> Of being in a hurry gone. We ran
> Behind the backs of houses, crossed a street
> Of blinding windscreens, smelt the fish-dock; thence
> The river's level drifting breadth began,
> Where sky and Lincolnshire and water meet.

There is an excitement of accidental seeing, accidental participation, which seems almost out of proportion to what is seen until we come to something more crucial: the wedding parties that (Whitsun being, one gathers, a traditional time to get married in England) repeat themselves at every station along the line. Now we see that "traveler" is, as in Elizabeth Bishop's poems, a metaphor for bachelor, outsider, voyeur—the non-participant who is granted a vision hidden from those inside society's normal covenants of connection. The vision, in this case, has to do with the endless repetitiveness of what is, for each participant, a unique moment. Such a vision can be one of annihilating pathos and vanity, expressed, in Larkin, comically, as a reduction of individuals to stock types:

> The fathers with broad belts under their suits
> And seamy foreheads; mothers loud and fat;
> An uncle shouting smut; and then the perms,
> The nylon gloves and jewellery-substitutes

But it can also be a vision of dense, fertile plenitude, as in Whitman. Larkin's penultimate stanza—and especially its wonderful concluding image—holds the two possibilities, fullness and emptiness, in an exquisite balance:

> and for
> Some fifty minutes, that in time would seem
>
> Just long enough to settle hats and say
>   *I nearly died*
> A dozen marriages got under way.
> They watched the landscape, sitting side by side
> —An Odeon went past, a cooling tower,
> And someone running up to bowl—and none
> Thought of the others they would never meet
> Or how their lives would all contain this hour.
> I thought of London spread out in the sun,
> Its postal districts packed like squares of wheat.

Christopher Ricks has faulted these lines, rather literalistically (how does *he* know "none / Thought of the others"?). But I think Larkin can be forgiven, in such a beautiful passage, for slightly overdrawing the contrast between insider and outsider. In any case, he chooses to end on a seemingly quieter note:

> it was nearly done, this frail
> Travelling coincidence; and what it held
> Stood ready to be loosed with all the power
> That being changed can give. We slowed again,

> And as the tightened brakes took hold, there swelled
> A sense of falling, like an arrow-shower
> Sent out of sight, somewhere becoming rain.

The first pleasure one gets from this ending is the surface pleasure of something exactly described: the strange vertiginous sensation of a train stopping. (Though in a poem so dense with, and about, the luxurious puzzlement of moving forward in life, no pleasure is just surface pleasure.) Later we feel how well the paradox of swelling and falling, crescendo and closure, fits our sense of such decisive settlements as weddings. And then we notice how graphically and movingly sexual it is, pointing to what has so far been left out of this account of how "A dozen marriages got under way." And that the child's rhyme

> I shot an arrow into the air
> It fell to earth I know not where

somehow comes into it. And that there is the potential of grief and tears—as well as fertility—as well as evanescence—in the "somewhere becoming rain." Like most truly magical moments in poetry, it is almost beyond paraphrase; but a large part of it is the sense of individual destiny at once enlarged and frighteningly lost in archetypal destiny, as when Randall Jarrell looks at his "Girl in a Library" and sees

> Firm, fixed forever in your closing eyes,
> The Corn King beckoning to his Spring Queen.

Neither Jarrell's poem nor Larkin's is a mystical one; but both have a feeling-tone akin to Whitman's pantheism, alongside their human sense of limitation and terror.

The thinking of the body is a rhythmical thinking. So it is hard to talk for long about Larkin's emotional depth without also talking about the fact that he is a great metrist. In particular, he is one of the great modern masters of the pentameter line; and it is within that line that, like Frost, he achieves his grand successes in bringing together high and low style, inwardness and observation, the moving "imprecisions" of speech and the deep "decisions" of "our flesh." (To which one should only add that, being twentieth-century poets, Larkin and Frost both show their mastery of pentameter most in their calculated and expressive violations of it.)

With all this in mind, I should like to look at some technical details of "Faith Healing"—a smaller-scale poem than "The Whitsun Weddings," but like it a poem of compassion, distance, and sexuality. "Faith Healing" begins so briskly, almost reportorially, that it is easy at first to overlook technique entirely: not to see how ingeniously Larkin uses enjambment, strong or weak caesura, a regular or a slightly ruffled flow of iambs, to make us feel emotionally frustrated, caught up short, left dangling, or, conversely, moved forward with a suspect ease. (The very fact that we do not know that it is going to be a rhymed poem until the fourth line—a line that itself moves compellingly forward toward a dubious, poignant, much-yearned-for goal—is part of the ingenuity.)

> Slowly the women file to where he stands
> Upright in rimless glasses, silver hair,
> Dark suit, white collar. Stewards tirelessly
> Persuade them onwards to his voice and hands,
> Within whose warm spring rain of loving care
> Each dwells some twenty seconds. *Now, dear child,*
> *What's wrong,* the deep American voice demands,
> And, scarcely pausing, goes into a prayer
> Directing God about this eye, that knee.
> Their heads are clasped abruptly; then, exiled
>
> Like losing thoughts, they go in silence; some
> Sheepishly stray, not back into their lives
> Just yet; but some stay stiff, twitching and loud
> With deep hoarse tears.

The enjambments at and just after the stanza break—each just following or preceding a particularly strong caesura—are especially powerful, leaving us, like the women, uncertain where to go, in limbo at the very moment fulfillment was promised. (The delayed rhyme of "exiled" with "*child*" helps—in the same way the delayed first rhyme did.) As the poem moves more deeply into the women's inner state, Larkin begins to do strange things with meter—triple stress-groups ("deep hoarse tears") and what Gerald Manley Hopkins called counterpoint, the inversion of the expected meter for several feet in a row:

> Thĕir thíck tŏngues blórt, thĕir eýes squéeze gríef, ă crówd
> Ŏf húge ŭnhéard ánswĕrs jăm ănd rejóice—

What the form imitates is less an emotion than a physiological state, "jammed" and constricted by the very intensity of release. (The word "blort"—which is found in no dictionary, but whose obvious puns are "bloat" and "blurt"—catches this perfectly.)

Having achieved this intense identification with the women, and then left us—with a stanza break on a dash—in the expectation of crisis, Larkin does something very histrionic and very successful. He repeats the evangelist's question in his own voice; and then, before answering it, intrudes a cruel and disheartening external "take" on the women, suggesting how unlovable they seem even to him:

> What's wrong! Moustached in flowered frocks they shake:
> By now, all's wrong.

It is a kind of effect of pacing which criticism easily overlooks or condescends to—but which in fact often gives poems (or novels, or movies) a good deal of their power over our emotions. In this case, it permits Larkin a suddenly rather vulnerable, inward, thinking-things-through tone of voice:

> In everyone there sleeps
> A sense of life lived according to love.
> To some it means the difference they could make
> By loving others, but across most it sweeps
> As all they might have done had they been loved.

I suspect this element of halting, nearly commonplace generality (in the midst of his great lyric gifts) makes Larkin a peculiarly trustworthy poet for many readers. Rhyme and meter make the thought feel serious enough; violations of meter make its emphases feel sincere:

$$\breve{A} \text{ sén}\acute{s}e \text{ ŏf líf\v{e} livéd áccórdĭng tŏ lóve.}$$

Of special importance, in such passages, are certain key words, strategically placed, that bring the largest lyrical world of the poem into the argument. So "sweeps," here, brings in the gusty, rainy early spring landscapes which in this poem (as, though the comparison seems odd, in *The Waste Land*) stand for the spirit's hesitant venture from the protective world of repression into the immensely testing and unguaranteeing world of admitted need:

> An immense slackening ache,
> As when, thawing, the rigid landscape weeps

It is, again, the physiological truth—the body, as well as the spirit, still armored, in Wilhelm Reich's sense, against the vulnerabilities it is starting to express—that makes the traditional metaphor so great here, and so hopeless. (And an echo of the jamming clusters of strong stresses—"immense slackening," "when, thawing"—comes back to remind us how that condition has already been embodied in the metrics of the poem.)

The hopelessness, of course, also arises from the miserable swindle which is the occasion for all this feeling; and the concluding movement of the poem, taken as a whole, both underlines this—by completing the echo "What's wrong" has begun—and subsumes it into something more universal:

> An immense slackening ache,
> As when, thawing, the rigid landscape weeps,
> Spreads slowly through them—that, and the voice above
> Saying *Dear child*, and all time has disproved.

It is only on a second reading, perhaps, that one sees clearly that the last line is an apposition: that "*Dear child*" is, or is part of, "all time has disproved." The longings awakened are precisely the childish ones—to be uniquely cherished, to be taken care of no matter what one is or does—that all experience, not just this particularly callous and cruel experience, is bound to disappoint. (And again one cannot help pausing, with awe and a little pedantry, to consider rhyme: how "disproved" picks up "love," "loved," and "above," the opening out of the vowel a mirror reversal of the closing down of the hope the other words imply. A whole essay could be written on the genius of Larkin's endings, the syntactic double takes, the unexpected twists of meter and rhyme—tricks that justify themselves by becoming revelations.)

It is no accident, I realize, that all of my examples so far come from Larkin's middle volume, *The Whitsun Weddings.* It is the apogee of his rueful—yet dark, sexy, almost pantheistic—fondness for humanity in the aggregate. It also has the richest, and best integrated, mix of his various styles—though that mix is already there in the great poems of *The Less Deceived,* "Church Going," "Myxomatosis," "Deceptions." The early work leads up to it, from surprisingly pure, lyrical beginnings, preserved in *The North Ship,* and even in certain Audenesque passages from the second book:

> Latest face, so effortless
> Your great arrival at my eyes,
> No one standing near could guess
> Your beauty had no home till then;
> Precious vagrant, recognise
> My look, and do not turn again.

(It may be that all great astringent poets are failed lyrists, seeking some underground outlet for an urgency that did not seem original enough, undisguised.)

Late Larkin is a more painful, and a more interesting, matter. The warmth toward humanity is mostly gone, replaced, it sometimes seems, mainly by a curmudgeonly, defensive fondness for things English. What is valuably, though disturbingly, new is a kind of exuberantly outrageous satire, whose complexity of effect has yet to be adequately appreciated. Robert

Pinsky has had the courage to point out, in his review of Larkin's prose book, *Required Writing,* what a crudely anti-American and anti-Semitic poem "Posterity" is. But Pinsky does not stop to ponder how and why Larkin enjoys the notion of his own life being written by "Jake Balokowsky, my biographer," and uses Balokowsky to deliver an utterly damning judgment on himself which, other poems suggest, is quite seriously meant. (Still, it is curious, reading through the volume *Larkin at Sixty,* to see how many friendly and utterly unembarrassed jokes about Balokowsky crop up. The British have a strange sense of entitlement to their prejudices—as if that were what Fate had given them in exchange for Empire.)

But if we look at a poem less clearly calculated to offend, we may be better able to see the peculiar, self-lacerating circularity of the whole maneuver. "Annus Mirabilis" starts:

> Sexual intercourse began
> In nineteen sixty-three
> (Which was rather late for me)—
> Between the end of the *Chatterley* ban
> And the Beatles' first LP.

We think we understand the conservative joke we're being asked to share, under the wistful banter: those young fools don't think anyone ever fucked before! But with the second stanza, the rhymes feel tighter, the picture gets vivid and serious:

> Up till then there'd only been
> A sort of bargaining,
> A wrangle for a ring,
> A shame that started at sixteen
> And spread to everything.

And suddenly we realize that in a sense the fools are right: the shame, and the stale situation comedy going on over it, did not deserve to be called sex, much less love. So that a genuine wonder and hope come into the beginning of the third stanza, only to be cut off again by a—this time slightly too pat—tightening of the rhyme:

> Then all at once the quarrel sank:
> Everyone felt the same,
> And every life became
> A brilliant breaking of the bank,
> A quite unlosable game.

And then the first stanza comes back, lighthearted and enigmatic as a song refrain, but with one or two slight changes that make all the difference:

> So life was never better than
> In nineteen sixty-three
> (Though just too late for me)—
> Between the end of the *Chatterley* ban
> And the Beatles' first LP.

Life is, indeed, "never better than" at the moment of untested change; but that is not the same as saying life is good. The young and the old fools are both right in their condemnations, wrong only in their confident hopes. And the poem—while it is significantly about sex, about cultural change, and about Larkin's personal sense of failure—is in the largest and most devastating sense about the vanity of the human wish for perfection.

The poem that best combines the peculiar strengths of these late satiric pieces with the visionary and imagistic strength of the ending of "The Whitsun Weddings" is "High Windows." (It is an indication of Larkin's self-critical acuteness that both are title poems.) The poem begins with the same kind of outrageous double take on changing mores that Larkin so obviously enjoys in "Annus Mirabilis":

> When I see a couple of kids
> And guess he's fucking her and she's
> Taking pills or wearing a diaphragm,
> I know this is paradise

Then it suddenly occurs to him that even *his* destiny might have seemed "paradise" to someone brought up in an even stricter old order:

No God any more, or sweating in the dark

About hell and that, or having to hide
What you think of the priest. He
And his lot will all go down the long slide
Like free bloody birds.

Does it enter into our reaction to these lines that "free" birds normally go up, not down; and that if they did go down a slide they might end up "bloody" in more than the colloquial British sense? There is a subtle glide here from the demotic into surrealism, that prepares us for the otherwise unexpected, and justly famous, concluding image:

And immediately

Rather than words comes the thought of high windows:
The sun-comprehending glass,
And beyond it, the deep blue air, that shows
Nothing, and is nowhere, and is endless.

The image is so vivid and haunting that one immediately believes Larkin's plain statement that it comes involuntarily, "Rather than words"; yet in fact it has as precise a logic as an Elizabethan conceit. As the "high windows" seem to hold only the sky, so experience remote enough in time comes to mirror the infinite, boundless possibility, "paradise." (If one imagines, as I always have, that the viewer is outside, looking up at the windows, which therefore reflect the sky, and hide what is actually behind them, the metaphor is even more perfect; but it also works if one assumes, as most readers seem to, that the viewer is inside, looking out.) The language of the stanza holds us in a wonderful equivocation as to whether there is any object for our yearning for original sources, boundless satisfactions. The "glass" "comprehends" the "sun," in the double sense of "understands" and merely "includes"; the scientific fact that the blue of the sky "is nowhere" is set against the empirical perception that it is "endless" and "deep." The feeling at the end is of self-surrender to what is utterly beyond us; but the tone of that feeling hovers between hope, poignancy, and a bleak awe.

Is Larkin in some sense a religious poet? Seamus Heaney's essay "The Main of Light"—of all the essays on Larkin, the one most responsive to the grandeur in his poetry—argues for a constant tension between his "anti-heroic, chastening, humanist voice" and "visionary moments" which express a yearning for "a more crystalline reality," "the world of the *Paradiso*." Heaney seems to me in the largest way right, and in a subtle way wrong. The danger is that the evocation of this hierarchy ascending toward traditional luminousness will simplify away from Larkin's work a more restrained but more unique timbre. The lines from "Solar" that Heaney quotes as unabashedly religious in tone (though "nothing . . . that the happy atheist could not accept") seem to me as moving as they are because—as with the end of "High Windows"—the tone is so sliding and equivocal:

> Coined there among
> Lonely horizontals
> You exist openly.
> Our needs hourly
> Climb and return like angels.
> Unclosing like a hand,
> You give forever.

It is the melancholy or neutral words that withdraw any easy anthropomorphism, easy consolation—"Coined," "lonely," "exist," "needs"—that give so much power to the final sense of an abiding generosity in mere existence.

Larkin remains a poet of limits, not of arrivals. The great moments in his poetry lead us to a feeling about First Things—dark and fertile in the case of "The Whitsun Weddings," beautiful but annihilating in the case of "High Windows"—beyond which he does not invite us (probably does not think it possible) to peer intellectually. One feels he would agree profoundly with Levin's discovery at the end of *Anna Karenina* that it is right for us to think of the sky as a round blue bowl, because that is what we see; though he would not agree at all with Tolstoy's corollary that we should accept conventional beliefs on the same basis.

To acknowledge this is to make Larkin a sadder, and a less philosophically ambitious, poet than Heaney suggests; but it also allows us to see that his more-than-rational grandeur attaches to his dark vision as well as to the luminous moments. And that both are inextricably woven into the fabric of his human and social perceptions. Let me take one final and particularly stunning example, from "Vers de Société." The poet has started to refuse an invitation to a boring party: "*Dear Warlock-Williams: I'm afraid—*" Then the reasons for his own fear of solitude begin to crowd in on him, until finally

> Beyond the light stand failure and remorse
> Whispering *Dear Warlock-Williams: Why, of course—*.

It's a little wicked to tease Larkin's shade on the score of his famous dislike of foreign poetry, but how completely that majestic first line could belong to the great last Baudelaire, the Baudelaire of "Recueillement" or "Le Voyage." One can hardly resist trying to jockey it into an alexandrine:

> *Au delà de la lampe le guignon, le remords . . .*

The last line is pure Betjeman, but without his clubby, in-joke self-consciousness. And they rhyme, with a grace and ease itself tragicomic. It seems a marvel that such a couplet could be written at all; and yet, once written, utterly natural. It is a little emblem of how the best poetry can make conventions seem silly in the dividing lines they lay down across territories wholly contiguous in the mind and in life. Larkin's poetry is the more remarkable because it makes the connections it does without avant-gardist showiness, and with so much grandeur, lucidity, and music salvaged from the high lyric traditions. He is one of the oddest, but I think one of the most clearly durable, successes of the art in English in the last half of the twentieth century.

Between Two Worlds

The Poetry of Eleanor Ross Taylor

For a devoted minority of readers, the preeminent woman poet in the senior generation might be—not any of the predictable choices, but a reticent Southerner, who prefers needlework and gardening to the reading circuit, and who has lived for more than forty years with her husband in such university towns as Charlottesville, Greensboro, Sewanee, and Gainesville. Eleanor Taylor's poetry has been notoriously hard to come by. Her first volume, lavishly praised by Randall Jarrell, was unavailable because of copyright difficulties for many years. Her *New and Selected Poems* (1983) came out with the small Southern publisher Stuart Wright, and was reviewed in almost no major periodicals. Now the University of Utah Press Poetry Series has remedied all that, bringing together eighty-some pages of new work, plus a generous selection from all three previous volumes.

After such praise, it may be best to begin with a poem. Here is "New Girls," from the 1983 volume:

> Devious, devious are
> primroses in shade
> collecting sunshine
> without sunshine.
> Sprawling on the grass
> they grip their books.

Review of *Days Going / Days Coming Back* by Eleanor Ross Taylor (Salt Lake City: University of Utah Press, 1991), from *American Poetry Review* 21, no. 6 (November–December 1992).

The strings of summer
ring without answer.
Hello Juliana?
Hello Augusta?
What are you doing tomorrow?
Sleeping,
          sleeping.

Numerous the shades
under primroses,
shifting sands and
sets and seasons,
reaching for the
fellow pillow,
reaching for the
strings of summer,
too treble, too shining
for inside eyes.

Yet this poem, like many of Taylor's, is so utterly itself that I almost despair of persuading anyone to like it, who doesn't like it instantly. I suppose I could begin with the comparisons. The shade-loving plants, "collecting sunshine / without sunshine," and the mysterious sexual plenitude of the girls who spend the whole summer day "Sleeping, / sleeping." The "strings" the plants hook onto to grow, and the girls' telephone cords. The pathos and child-sensuality of the "fellow pillow." The wonderful *names*. Then I might point to the music. It was Randall Jarrell who first compared Eleanor Taylor's poetry to Thomas Hardy's, and the comparison fits these short lines, irregular at first, gathering to a sing-songy trochaic dimeter at the very point where the leaps of association become strangest ("shifting sands and / sets and seasons"). Finally this music becomes the music of the girls' lives, and invokes itself, defying the reader to condescend: "too treble, too shining / for inside eyes." If this poem was modeled on John Crowe Ransom's exquisite, outmoded lyric "Blue Girls," it is a much tenderer, because more empathetic, elegy for what youth doesn't have—and for what it does.

The Hardy comparison is, of course, apt to much else as

well. One thinks of his "wistlessness" and "norward," encountering the inimitable oddities that sparkle, like mica, through Taylor's lines and titles. The cross "ethered up" above the altar. "[S]he mollusks somewhere." "In the Echoes, Wintering." Like Hardy, she cherishes a rural, dialect culture, all the more tenderly the more powerless it seems in the face of urban cosmopolitanism; yet, like him, she never forgets the distortions it wreaked on individual yearnings for freedom, when it had power. Like him, too, she can never quite let go of Christianity, or of the dread of the void after death, the ghostliness cast back over life, that comes with the fading of literal belief. There is even a trace of his troubled erotic naturalism in "Harvest, 1925," a period piece about a farm woman taken in adultery,

> weeping, behind the plums,
> a lactate field mouse,
> shucks cleaving
> to her teats.

Both are poets caught "between two worlds," in Matthew Arnold's phrase, never quite able to prefer the modern, secular, permissive one, yet sharing its perspectives.

Eleanor Taylor once wrote a rather notorious bad review of Sylvia Plath's *Ariel*. (She did make a prescient exception for some of the quieter poems, "Elm," "A Birthday Present," "Totem.") Reading some of her own early poems like "Goodbye Family," it's easy to feel that Plath's brand of suicidal individualism, the "White Godiva" unpeeling all the claims of others, "Dead hands, dead stringencies," was for her a road not taken:

> The years to climb! The walls to catch at!
>   To cut free
> And drop through the cloak closet and cellar
>   Is better—
> Under the foundations of God's world
>   Lilily
> Swimming on my side, with ear on shoulder,
>   Eyes unlettered,

And intellectuality an asterisk
    Now blurred—
It's no use God's whistling, "Come back, Fido,
    Come back,
I won't tease any more." I'm in the glade
    Remembering
I meant to tell my daughter, "I looked for
    You a cattail
But they were all silked out—"
    And now the water
Meeting me around the curve, roaring, blanks
    Out all but ear:
        Not in the day time, not in the dark time
        Will my voice cut and my poison puff
        My treasures of flesh
        My gems of flashing translucent spirit,
        Nor my caress shatter them.

That primal unity, "Under the foundations," where such musical tautologies as "Lilily" can happen; that lyric, suicidal escape, fueled as much by self-hatred, hatred of the "poison" hidden even in the frustrated ego's brilliance and kindness, as by resentment of others—all that would, some years later, be Plath's temptation, the "cauldron of morning" in which the "I" and everything else is melted down at the end of "Ariel."

For Eleanor Taylor, it is a rare mood, after *Wilderness of Ladies*. In her transitional volume, *Welcome Eumenides*, some poems even fly to the opposite extreme of unambivalent moral conservatism ("The Young Writer's Reply"). But in the poems of her prolific late flowering, from about 1974 on, her vision remains double, examining with anger and fierce empathy the spiritual lives of those who do not flee their backgrounds, or the constraints of family and class. Consider "When Robins Return," an elegy for an "eccentric," mother-dominated bachelor who wished to be reincarnated as a bird:

    I wonder when I hear at dawn in May
    that volubility at serious play
    whether it's born verbal charm to tempt
    earthworms, his Methodist constraint to pray. . . .

I see him flying with his lady mother
south, falls, to the Gulf. They doff their feathers
(at last she thinks him lyrical and bold)
evenings under magnolia weather,

play two-hand bridge, shuffling the red and black
cards with goldish talons. The fatal pack
is marked a different way this go-around:
justly, he'll eat her while she's fighting back.

How delicately this poem appreciates the man, while telling all of the terrible unspoken truths about his life! How delicately, too, it handles all of the familiar tropes—nature as freedom, as what might absolve, in "serious play," the constrictions, the half-aggressions, half-deceptions of our socially warped selves; and against that the wish that that exact self could be held on to, could even get its own "back," for life's humiliations . . . It seems to me another near-perfect lyric, extending but deepening the line of Hardy and Ransom.

Taylor's characters are often victims, but her loyalties are too stubborn, too complex, for them ever to be the predictable, "politically correct" ones. Perhaps that is why two of her most ambitious poems, "Rachel Plummer's Dream" and "War Paint and Camouflage," seem to draw on those supremely unfashionable texts in which white settlers are the victims of Native Americans, not the other way around.

Rachel Plummer seems an almost inhuman extension of the "ladylike" virtues of avoiding self-pity, taking an interest in the world, until they become artist-virtues, mystic virtues. "You never shut your eyes. / You always looked"—even when her husband and baby are brutally slaughtered. And she goes on noting it all down, in her copybook prose, "the Purest Are you ever breathed," "the Fine Springs, the Snow Rabbitt." She insists on being admitted to the Indian culture ("a dog that *would*"), though she draws certain lines: "refused the serving of roast enemy; it was a foot." (This is no *Dances with Wolves*, where the real atrocities are always committed by some other tribe.) And it is, finally, her need to "see" that makes her rebel violently, as she has not, of course, at any of her real torments. When her young Indian "mistress" is afraid to explore a mountain cave with her, Rachel beats the woman, then leads her "the miles back to the mouth," and then, alone,

> at last made your long way in that unearthly
> twinkling dark, beside the crystal river,
> to sound of mighty falls ahead,
> > > plunging
> how far? into what unknown place?
> > caught echoes of your dying baby's cries;
> like tranced Ezekiel in Babylon
> > descried the noise of wings, of wings let down—
> *though briers and thorns be with thee, not afraid!*

What we know—though Rachel perhaps does not—is that "this parapsychologic episode" appropriates the form of a young Indian male's vision-quest. Yet the content of her self-healing is Christian, and, what is more, patriarchal. For all the powerfully feminist implications of inner space, caves, the waterfall vanishing into uncharted depth, it is a "He," a divine father/lover, who at last comes "to bathe / your wounds that never pained again." (In her own, first-person, attempt to "analyze," Taylor writes "I discount sex," making one at once love her brashness—not unlike Plummer's own—and feel she has missed the whole point of psychoanalytic thinking, if she thinks "sex" is separable from such other fundamental needs as nurturance and recognition.) In the end, Taylor seems to opt for Plummer's own, literally Christian explanation—

> that Resurrection flaring in the cave,
> those stars in earth, time stopped
> and you with eyes to see.

I think it is because Rachel Plummer's triumph fits no category that is entirely comfortable for the late twentieth-century reader, that it sticks so undislodgeably, at least in my mind. In her quiet way, Rachel is a challenge to all of those texts that would see nothing but a humiliating "identification with the oppressor" in the perversely complex loyalties women have shown, over the centuries. Beyond even gendered considerations, she becomes a kind of savage parable of the spirit, creating itself out of irreconcilable contradiction, out of what compromises, tortures, or violates it, because that is what it means to exist in space and time.

In the more recent poem, "War Paint and Camouflage" (when it first appeared in the *New Yorker,* it was called, more simply and movingly, "Captive Voices"), no such heroic transcendence seems possible. For these captives, "Mountains were never sublime and / forests did not breathe grandeur," because

> Raising the eyes and looking far
> requires a certain off-guard.
> Requires if not pleasure in, some
> concord with one's status quo.

The voices of real captivity, real torture, are juxtaposed, in the *Waste Land* manner, with contemporary voices. The risk is that the latter will simply be annihilated by the comparison. (One of them actually says, "People *suffered,*" speaking of a five-day power outage.) Yet many of these voices are so inventive, so gifted with words—

> Well, the doctor didn't want me to become addicted.
> So it was Tantalus all over again, with the Tylenol

or

> You see two people were needed:
> somebody to take Dad to the hospital
> and somebody to stay with Mom.
> That's why it happened—
> I couldn't be two people

—that in the end they force our compassion, force us to acknowledge the common human denominators—pain, the fear of death, the desire to have enough under control for "a certain off-guard." Even this paper world approaching the millennium, where "The hunger of the first part / sues the hunger of the second part," is as it is because "hunger," in all its senses, is fundamental and increasing. The poem ends with

what can either be another abrupt voice, with an unexpect-
edly sharp cut at the pro-lifers (yes, you never are quite sure
of the politics here), or, in dead earnest, the author's "prayer":

> I carry my prayer on a stick:
> Over-population is murder.

Given her empathy for trapped lives, given, also, her peren-
nially divided perspective on historical change, it is small won-
der that Taylor is one of the great contemporary elegists.
Besides "When Robins Return," and the cryptic but heart-
breaking elegy for Jarrell, "New Dust," I would recommend
the family elegies, especially "Dry Nights," "Rack and Ruin,"
and "Limits." And then, in the odder genre of self-elegy—
poems that try to come to terms with the poet's own blank
future—"Pain in the House" and "Next Year," which ends a
catalog of seemingly optimistic predictions with

> I won't miss the ducks' migration:
> stepping into the night by my gate I'll hear
>   the appointed skytramping,
> the comradely call; who knows?
> it may be my year to share
>   the vacant eye full of destination.

One could go on quoting forever; nearly every poem has at
least one or two such stunning effects as "skytramping," or
that "vacant"/"full" last line. But let me conclude, instead, with
a mild complaint, at the omission of the longest and best of
the family elegies from the Stuart Wright volume, "The Rib-
bon to Norwood." Reliving a long, slow bus trip to visit the
poet's dying mother, the poem somehow subsumes the whole
story of Southern womanhood, back to the stockade at James-
town, that has been the burden of so much of Taylor's work.
At a climactic point, the poem shifts to dialect, the quintessen-
tial mother tongue:

> *Goin Yanceyville*
> *Don think my mama goin live very long.*
>   In her voice, some-old-lonesome

> freight train whooping at the crossing.
> Will this loosestrife live?
>   Now hit's a wild thing,
>   a wild thing used to do-without.
> To make them live. To hold them back.
> They pull me on.

"Hit," here, appears to be the dying mother's spirit; but it could equally well be the suicidal wife of "Goodbye Family," or the anonymous maker of "The Altar Needlework," or Rachel Plummer, or the poet herself. "Hit" is the new note, proud and solitary, yet in its very elusiveness somehow reconciling the claims of detachment and allegiance, that Eleanor Ross Taylor has added to the poetry of American women, and to American poetry per se.

II

Montale and the Screen of Images

The question of how and why images succeed in poems is a vexing one. In an article of faith that extends from the Imagists to Robert Bly, the image is the vivid, sensuous, ineluctably particular element that makes the poem a reenactment, rather than an intellectual reduction, of life. But in my own experience, both as poet and reader, the effect of vividness in fact depends on a changing chemistry between the image and other poetic elements: syntax, meter, lineation; the speaking voice; the explicitly meditative or discursive sides of the poem. Monotonous modes of presentation, or modes that too automatically presume that the image is valuable because it *is* an image, can deaden even great virtues of observation or symbolic resonance. It seems to me trivializing to regard this merely as a problem of conventions and the need to vary them. I have to believe, and intuitively do believe, that the labor of stationing the image has its own subject matter, lodged in the psychology of our attachment to visual things, and in the ontological status that our metaphysics—conscious or unconscious—assigns to them. For the great imagistic poet, nothing is more fundamental than the psychic or philosophical relation to the image; and the poem is at least as much concerned with that relation as with any virtue the image has in and of itself.

No writer I have studied in recent years has been more helpful with these problems than the great Italian poet Eugenio Montale. It is not merely that Montale is (at least in the central volumes *Le Occasioni* and *La Bufera*) a radically imagistic poet who sometimes baffles me but never loses my interest.

Parnassus 13, no. 2 (spring–summer 1986).

Nor is it merely that some of his poems contain a searching epistemological inquiry into the satisfactions images provide, or fail to provide, in our mental lives. Rather it is that such an inquiry is felt, throughout his poetry, in the variations of emotional texture as the actual images slide, crowd, or majestically preempt their way into the poem.

To put the matter most paradoxically, I do not think Montale would be as great an imagistic poet as he is if he did not have so strong a capacity to hate the image, and yearn for the imageless. In the early poem *Forse un mattino*, the air through which we perceive the normal world is "arid" and "glassy," and "the miracle," the moment of revelation, would be the disappearance of everything. I know of no adequate translation of this poem, so I offer my own:

> Perhaps, out walking one morning in the arid
> glassy air, I will turn and see the miracle—
> nothing at all behind me, the void
> touching my shoulders—with a drunkard's terror.
>
> And then, as if on a screen, they will slide back effortlessly
> houses trees hills in the usual deception.
> But it will be too late; and I will go silently,
> among the men who have never turned round, hugging my
> secret.

The "drunkard's terror" notwithstanding, the attitude toward this "miracle" seems primarily one of eager expectation. When the world returns, it is a "screen" (*schermo*) with all that implies both of falsity and of interference, concealment. The truth lies with annihilation; to see the world at all is to become part of a vaguely demeaning social conspiracy ("usual" can also read "customary").

The screen, the chain, the net, the "prism of the minute" in which the "living . . . lose their way," like white light broken into its colors, in "Times at Bellosguardo"—Montale's poetry offers many images for this essentially Manichaean vision of the world of multiplicity as an illusion, a trap. Most of these images particularly emphasize the quality of seamlessness— the endless superficies in which every object is connected to every other but no object is more important than any other. This effect is marvelously conveyed by the unpunctuated strings of nouns, "houses trees hills" in the poem quoted above, or, in "Arsenio," the "street porch walls mirrors" that "fixes you"—the verb is significantly singular in the Italian— "in a single frozen multitude of the dead."[1]

The theme has a moral as well as an epistemological dimension; Arsenio's "chain" is his "motionless motion," the seamless passage of life in which choices are made for us by habit, psychological pattern, possibility, without our being conscious of ever having actually chosen. For this range of meanings, Montale tends toward an imagery of insensate vegetative growth: "the spores of the possible" in "News from Amiata," the seaweed of "The Dead" whose linking "strands" are at once the heart's prison and the history of its choices or failures to choose, "whatever once stopped / in us resigned to its cage." In both contexts—moral and epistemological—there is the same contrast between the single significant moment, the "instant . . . long wished-for" of "Arsenio," and the indivisible superficies, the "delirium . . . of immobility."

And yet, Montale is always ambivalent about the possibility, even the desirability, of breaking the chain. He wishes for the singular moment, "in which things yield and seem / about to betray their ultimate secret," as eagerly as did those other great Romantics and Symbolists who called it a "spot of time," an "epiphany," a "*correspondence.*" In that moment, when the gap is closed between appearance and essence, and the world becomes a transparent symbol, lies the possibility of a knowledge that is not Manichaean, that is neither "void" nor "screen." But Montale insists, in the central early poem *I limoni,* that such a moment would be

> a mistake of nature,
> the dead point of the world, the link which will not hold,
> the thread to disentangle which might set us at last
> in the midst of a truth.

These lines often, and understandably, remind readers of the lines written a decade and a half later by T. S. Eliot:

> At the still point of the turning world. Neither flesh nor
>   fleshless;
> Neither from nor towards; at the still point, there the dance
>   is,
> But neither arrest nor movement. And do not call it fixity

But the difference between Eliot's profoundly Christian vision and Montale's seems finally more important than the similarity. One can conceivably experience a "still point" of the world, and see the life of "flesh" there doubled and enhanced with its "fleshless" meaning. One cannot experience a "dead point," except as a disintegration, an absence; indeed, its very existence is ominously threatening to the world—"the link which will not hold." One cannot, for Montale, be "in the midst of a truth" and also in life. And so the epiphany becomes the willed act of "the mind" which "seeks harmonizes disunites" (another significantly unpunctuated string) in search of a unity of impression which must remain aesthetic, not ontological. At best, the epiphany is an unprovable intuition, that occurs too quickly to be grasped, or when we are slightly turned away from the natural object—as someone in an old orchard might hear a laborer departing and imagine he had scared away a satyr or Pan:

> Silences in which one sees
> in each departing human shadow
> some dislodged Divinity.

And yet, Montale's poetry does single out epiphanic images as much as—perhaps more than—most poetry does. For in the continuum, or screen of images, it is as undeniable that special moments occur as that they cannot be fathomed or held still. "It is too sad / that so much peace should gather only by glints" (from the first part of "Times at Bellosguardo") seems the quintessential Montalean statement about consciousness. And in fact, the poetic effect of Montale's skepticism is usually to drive him to an ever subtler and more specific delineation of the moments in which the surface has seemed about to give way, or the "glints" off of the surface to gather to "so much peace."

The poem of Montale's which has attracted the most attention and controversy by the cryptic specificity of its moment of discovery is the Sixth Motet. The poem deals with a separation from a beloved woman: it is *the* subject for Montale, the situation that over and over again draws forth his peculiar mixture of alienation and revelation, the "departing human shadow" becoming a "dislodged Divinity." The separation intensifies to a point of crisis the preexisting feeling that the world is a "screen of images" (the phrase in fact comes from the Sixth Motet), excluding the poet from some ultimate communion or truth. And yet the poet cannot help interpreting this "screen" as a system of "signs": "the signs of death" if it totally excludes and obliterates the memory of the beloved, or, alternatively, in however "distorted" and "labile" a form, a reminder, "a dazzle of you" (*un* tuo *barbaglio*). From this posing of alternatives the poem drops to its famous and, for many of its early readers, outrageously cryptic epiphany:

> (At Modena, between the porticoes,
> Came a liveried servant, dragging
> Two jackals on a leash).

The image, it seems to me, does not answer the question posed by the first half of the poem so much as it drags its alternatives together by force. Jackals, and the regalia of servitude, are certainly "signs of death." But the quality of extravagant, disdainful display echoes what is extreme, abrupt, showy in the beloved, her "dazzle"—as, in the Italian, the sounds of "dazzle" (*barbaglio*) echo through "liveried" (*gallonato*) and "jackals" (*sciacalli*) to come to rest, with the poem, with a full rhyme on "leash" (*guinzaglio*).

Montale's own explanation of this poem was devastatingly simple: "Clizia loved droll animals," therefore the jackals might have been a kind of occult sign, a troubadour's *senhal*, sent by her. And Rebecca West, in her excellent book on Montale, has noted the pivotal significance of the *barbaglio-guinzaglio* rhyme, and has seen in it the beginning of a whole symbolism of light and splendor surrounding Clizia in Montale's later poetry.[2] Nevertheless, I am inclined to stick with the overdetermined meaning the subsidiary rhymes suggest to me: that for the hopelessly devoted lover, who is often delineated, in the troubadours, by the word *servant*, the Lady's "dazzle" is both predatory and Enlightening, gives both life and death. The image suffices to bring the poem to rest because it includes, however subliminally, the opposing feelings that have been at war within the poem from the beginning. And Montale's skill as a poet is nowhere more evident than in the way he leaves the image accidental and given, part of the "screen"—by not explaining it, by putting it in parentheses—while at the same time leading the reader, by the gathering concentration of sound, to an intuition of its resolving force.

The same stringent, ascetic search for the satisfying image can stretch over an entire volume, if not the lifework. Clizia, the Lady of the *barbaglio,* dominates *La Bufera* by her perpetual departure from it, truly a "dislodged Divinity" there. Yet we learn only one thing about her physical appearance, and come to recognize her by it in poems where her presence would otherwise be in doubt. She has long bangs that cover her high forehead, and she repeatedly brushes or tosses them back:

> The way it was when
> you turned, your forehead brushed
> of a cloud of hair,
>
> and waved to me—and stepped into darkness.
>
> ("The Storm")

> Don't push back the strands of hair which veil
> your child-like forehead. They, too, speak
> of you—they are the whole sky wherever I go,
> my only light except for the jades
> which circle your wrist
>
> ("The Strands of Hair")

> and has a proud
> toss of the head that pushes back

from the forehead, from the burning eyes and thick
   eyebrows,
her childish wave of hair
                    ("Voice Arriving with the Coots")

The gesture is full of vitality and at the same time fruitless, circular. It expresses an endless impatience, with herself and perhaps with the conditions of material existence. It is an effort to disclose: to unveil the angelic, sexless, transcendental portion of herself, the "restless forehead" that "covers the dawn, and hides it." It is also an effort to get rid of what in her is mere personality—the dramatic feminine glamour which another side of her nevertheless desires. (She could cut her hair shorter; she could stop wearing jade.) In its combination of disclosure and repudiation, it is appropriately, as so many epiphanic gestures are in Montale, a gesture on the edge of darkness, a farewell. It is also "child-like"—a word that, from poem to poem, floats between the hair itself and the forehead, as if Montale recognized some common element of infantile yearning expressed both in Clizia's way of being attractive and in her religious absolutism, which intrigues and baffles him so much in *La Bufera*. Thus, as in the motet, Montale's intuition settles with compass-needle accuracy on the one image that seems right because it expresses all his conflicting perceptions and feelings; and then, with characteristic disdain for the images that are mere "screen," it rests, it does no more.

And yet, the image can function in an opposite way in Montale's poetry—by an endless proliferation, that dramatizes our entrapment in, and bafflement before, the screen. This results in another kind of poetic difficulty, a difficulty of clutter and undifferentiated listing—which does, however, often resolve into a marvelous suggestiveness. Consider, for instance, the short poem "A Metropolitan Christmas (London)," which seems to be about a more casual, but if anything more unhappy, love relationship:

> Mistletoe, from childhood a hanging cluster
> of faith and hoar-frost over your washstand
> and the oval mirror which your shepherd-curls
> now shade among the paper saints and photographs

of boys slipped helter-skelter into
the frame; an empty decanter,
small glasses of ashes and rinds,
the lights of Mayfair; later, souls at a crossing,
bottles which could not open themselves—
no longer war or peace; the final whirr
of a pigeon unable to follow you
on the escalator which slides you down.

This woman's appurtenances of glamour seem too multiple, empty, askew—allusions to faith, love, and sophistication beneath which the speaker senses mainly nostalgia for a childhood too recently left behind. The syntax drags these meager objects along in an endless bumping succession, like the *gradini automatici* ("automatic steps") of the escalator at the end. There is no punctuation stronger than a comma in the original; and the line breaks regularly divide subjects from objects, prepositional phrases from the nouns they modify. When the two people's "souls" enter the poem, they are caught, both syntactically and metaphorically, within the list. "Bottles which could not open themselves," they seem to belong on that washstand, grouped forever among the other "empty," "helter-skelter" objects which fail to "open" onto the meanings they suggest. (Our whole sense is of a mismatched, frustrating relationship; instead of moving from outdoors to indoors, to greater intimacy, the poem begins with the speaker ill at ease before the youthful sadness of the woman's room, then mysteriously driven outdoors, to leave her, finally, at the entrance to an Underground station.) The final image is wonderful: the impulse of ascent into a sky of love and freedom drawn helplessly (and futilely) down the "automatic steps" of the relationship and the poem, and itself taking on the comic and pathetic "whirr" of a machine. (It is also a sight every tourist has seen in London, and that, for whatever reason, one doesn't see much in other cities; you can be sure it pleased Montale to make the local coincide so perfectly with the symbolic.)

The deployment of syntax in this poem takes us back to what we said at the beginning about the moral dimension of

the image of the chain, of "motionless motion." We believe
we confront the world as a string of nouns; that the aspect of
spectacle, of mere will-less presence, looms endlessly larger,
at least temporally, than the moments of action or choice.
But we find that there are always hidden verbs; that the
nouns we set ourselves in front of, and our reaction to them,
put us somewhere we were not at the beginning and did not
necessarily want to be—like the speaker whose middle-aged
yearnings stand revealed to him in that sad, funny pigeon-
whirr. A more perfect example (in which the verbs do, in
fact, step forth like Wordsworth's pursuing mountain from
behind the seemingly innocent nouns) may be found in an-
other, perhaps the greatest, of Montale's Lost Lady poems,
"Dora Markus." The passage describes the kind of not-quite-
first-class resort where Dora is usually to be found, in the
company of one of "those men / with high, weak whiskers /
in the big, gold portraits." I quote it in Italian as well as in
English for an exact sense of how the grammar works in
counterpoint to the line breaks:

> The evening, extended
> over the humid inlet
> brings, with the buzzing of motors,
> only the cries of geese,
> and the snow-white porcelain
> interior, tells in the blackened
> mirror, that sees you changed,
> a story of cool mistakes
> etching it in with acid
> where the sponge can't reach.
>
> La sera che si protende
> sull'umida conca non porta
> col palpito dei motori
> che gemiti d'oche e un interno
> di nivee maioliche dice
> allo specchio annerito che ti vide
> diversa una storia di errori
> imperturbati e la incide
> dove la spugna non giunge.

From the beginning there are enjambments and postpone-
ments; verbs of promise (*si protende*) and of restriction (*non
porta . . . che*) are alike clouded by the intrusion of long descrip-
tive phrases. But the real surprises begin with the fourth line.
Un interno sounds as if it will conclude the list of objects the
evening brings; only when we reach *dice* at the end of the fifth
line do we realize that it begins a new clause, that the objects
"speak." The sixth and seventh lines contain a similar double
take; what seems a static relation ("the blackened mirror that
sees you") becomes, with the line break, a dynamic one ("that
sees you / changed"). And the surprises go on: the oxymoron
"cool mistakes" (*errori / imperturbati*) is similarly broken over
two lines, and the final "etching it in" (*e la incide*) is, in the
original, a further unexpected clause where the very length of
the sentence would lead one to anticipate a period. The moral
is clear: the seemingly static images, which reflect Dora's
"cool" presupposition that her life, if it goes nowhere, at least
stays under control, are torn away in a hidden syntactic flow
which is the flow of time made visible.

There is one extraordinary poem of Montale's in which the
infernal and the saving possibilities of the image are brought
face to face with each other, the second part of "Times at
Bellosguardo." The poem begins with Montale's most ex-
treme image of vegetative entrapment, the helplessly reflec-
tive magnolia leaf:

> Desolate, exposed
> on the low hill
> magnolia foliage: brownish-
> green if the wind carries
> with the ground-floor chill a distorted
> rushing of harmonies,
> and every leaf that vibrates
> and kindles in the thicket
> drinks to its last fibre
> the greeting; and more desolate
> the foliage of the living
> who lose their way
> in the prism of the minute

It is an image of consciousness as fixed in the world, yet unable to reach the world; unable to turn away either, and taking from its own subjective distortion and excitement the illusion that the world offers either "harmonies" or "greeting." It is the most terrible image of consciousness in all of Montale's poetry, and its sense of passive helplessness extends to the moral life as well. Our "acts" are "minutes mirrored," a ricochet of ever-changing circumstances embodied in an aurally circular line (*atti minuti specchiati*) whose grinding, battering music is quite typical of the poem, and extreme even for Montale. To "choose life"—the first grim, pessimistic movement of the poem concludes—is to consent to this endless, kaleidoscopic fragmentation of ourselves; it is thus "another death."

And yet the poem takes an unexpected and magnificent turn when it comes to the abiding past, the "galleries and herms" of the villa on Bellosguardo. As the present (*cuna*— alternately "cradle" or "vaulted ceiling") "descends" among these relics, "the harmony," which earlier was a mere "distorted rushing," seems to "draw in," as into a chord, almost to bring to life (*commuove*)

> the stones that have seen the great
> images, honor,
> inflexible love, the wager,
> faith that does not bend.

It is an odd, idiosyncratic list: perhaps "the wager" could be one of the "great images" only for a countryman of those princes who found the same mathematical beauty in outwitting an enemy as in sustaining a cathedral dome. But it is its presence in the list—along with the light oxymoron of "inflexible love"—that allows the magnificent equalizing indefiniteness of the poem's conclusion.

> And the gesture remains: to measure
> the emptiness, sound its boundaries:
> the obscure gesture that expresses
> itself and nothing else: the ever-living
> passion one blood, one brain

> that cannot be repeated; and perhaps it enters
> what closes us and forces it with a slender
> picklock's point.

The inflexible gestures, each of which "expresses / itself and nothing else," are the same as the great images—one wager, in which selfhood, or meaning, is laid down against the blind continuity of the physical and temporal universe. They express an impulse almost beyond time, an "ever-living passion" incarnate in "one blood, one brain / that cannot be repeated." Entering "what closes us," the world of seamless fixity and ignorance we share with the magnolia leaf, the gesture will "perhaps" (that "perhaps" which, as Rebecca West observes, is almost Montale's favorite word—but here it precedes the strongest religious affirmation in his poetry) "force" it to open onto its opposite, a boundless, transcendental dimension. It will do so, of course, not by assured right, like St. Peter's key, but illegitimately and almost by chance, "with a slender / picklock's point." (In the original, the near-identity of the words *forza*, "force," and *forse*, "perhaps," is a powerful element in the effect.)

This apologetic, ambiguous, almost guilty spirituality is one of the most difficult, and moving, components in Montale's poetic mix, and certainly the most unlike anything in our own tradition. It is as remote from the efforts to revive traditional or esoteric systems of thought in the great Modernists as it is from the gnosticism or negative theology that appeals to so many contemporary writers. Its object of devotion is the living energy of the individual, the miracle of our conscious presence—the gesture that expresses only itself, the blood and brain "that cannot be repeated." This energy has as many forms as there are people or, at least, cultural moments; yet—and this is the real article of faith—is everywhere equal, whether its projective force reaches to gods or only to the slightest, most subjective brightening of a few of the objects on the screen.

Perhaps the clearest and most concrete instance of this mode of devotion is the gigantic wager that sets Clizia's living energy against the entire reality of the Second World War in *La Bufera*. Clizia appears there, of course, as an exemplar of literal religious faith. But it is a faith admired, rather than shared, by the poet; in a very real sense, Clizia is to him as God is to her.

It is ambiguous, from the start, whether Clizia's presence in wartime Europe is literal, or entirely an inward gesture of the poet's imagination. The imagery of the poems often seems to suggest that she died a martyr's death in the war, perhaps in the Resistance, or in a bombing raid:

> It was easier to use oneself up, to die
> at the first beating of wings, at the first encounter
> with the enemy; that was child's play. Henceforth
> begins the harder path: but not you, eaten
> by sun, and rooted . . .
>   not you, fragile
> fugitive to whom zenith nadir cancer
> capricorn remains indistinct
> becausse the war was within you and within
> whoso adores upon you the wounds of your Spouse

Yet some of Montale's interviews suggest—and most of his commentators have presumed—that Clizia was three thousand miles away at the time, and present only as a beacon of hope in the poet's mind. Perhaps it doesn't matter: Clizia is a martyr in spirit, in her passionate identification with suffering, her desire to take the war within her in the all-inclusive expiatory act that will make her one with Christ. Her pantheistic mysticism assaults the normal boundaries that separate human beings from nature, from each other, and from God. Thus she becomes a kind of anti-self to Montale the skeptic, who cannot quite believe either that the screen of images will split apart in a moment of mystical revelation, or that the chain of history can be broken by a single heroic action. Montale distances himself from Clizia's faith, sometimes quite brutally ("the unlimited godhead / whose faithful it devours that it may feed them"). Yet his poetry needs the tension with her headlong commitment to attain the passionate fullness of voice that comes in *La Bufera*. She becomes, finally, his "great image" laid down against the nature of things, "what closes us," to transform or unlock it—"perhaps." And, indeed Montale speaks of her very much in these terms in a climactic passage from "The Orchard," half conceding that he has arbitrarily chosen to superimpose her on his own experience of the war years:

> O purpose exceeding your own compass, having formed
> the hands of the dial and expanding
> into human time, into human space, in rages
> of incarnate demons, in brows of angels
> sped down in flight

Clizia's "purpose," her *intento*, he says, has carried her beyond her "own compass"—perhaps meaning beyond the actual facts of her life—to inhabit, indeed to "form" a different, all-inclusive kind of moral space. It is a space where the real and the imaginary are curiously coextensive. It does not matter that the "incarnate demons" are real and external, the Nazis, whereas the angels are only a projection of Clizia herself—their brows, like hers, their only visible feature. The single, modern, undivided soul, by accepting the "inhuman anguish" and remaining "undivided," "expands" the world—without faith or dogma—to the full moral dimensionality of the *Divine Comedy*.

I do not think that Montale intends this reference to the very beginnings of his own tradition to go unnoticed. Indeed, I am convinced that Montale, when he returned to the *Motets* to find a heroine for his war poems, remembered very clearly how Dante too had written a little book, a "novellette" of love, parting, and the Platonic ladder, considered it complete in its own right, and then, in his years of suffering and exile, found its love story a sufficient fulcrum for a poem including all that he knew of political and moral good and evil. There is, of course, a definite hubris involved in comparing a sequence of lyrics, clearly agnostic, and containing only one, quite equivocal and fantastic, dramatic action—Clizia's martyrdom—with the master epic of Christian Europe. But it is perhaps no greater than Dante's own hubris in placing himself and Beatrice at the center of such an epic. Both testify to the sense that it is individual *intento*, the "gesture that expresses / itself and nothing else," rather than doctrine, that carries us over from "what closes us" to an infinitely expanded world. It is this conviction that makes Montale's lifelong struggle with the image serious, radical, and religious.

How far other poets, or even readers, can enter into what is effectively a private religion is perhaps a moot point. But for me, Montale is one of those writers who establish a kind of threshold in a particular domain of the art: a level of virtuosity which, once recognized, leaves one permanently and healthily uneasy with lesser goals. He shows that even a poem as small as the Sixth Motet can give an account—however compressed—of the ontological status it assigns to images in general, as well as of the emotional complex that makes a particular image inevitable. Having absorbed him, we cannot easily return to the touristic satisfaction with imagery per se that weakens so much contemporary American poetry. Yet he is no enemy of the image; rather, he inspires confidence in— and, if we are poets, suggests new ways of manifesting—the ineluctable centrality certain images have for us. Like most original geniuses, he brings both new severities and new enjoyments to our experience of art.

Notes

1. The passages from "Arsenio" and "Times at Bellosguardo" are, again, in my own renderings. (My version of "Times at Bellosguardo" appeared in *Canto* 4, no. 1 [June 1981].) All other quotations are taken from Eugenio Montale, *Selected Poems* (New York: New Directions, 1965).

2. See Rebecca J. West, *Eugenio Montale: Poet on the Edge* (Cambridge: Harvard University Press, 1981), 50–52, where Montale's own comment on the poem is quoted. Claire de C. L. Huffman, with whom I had the good fortune to study Montale in 1977, gives a reading closer to my own, though more searching than either mine or Rebecca West's, in her recent *Montale and the Occasions of Poetry* (Princeton: Princeton University Press, 1983).

Poetry and Politics (I)
The Case of Coming to Jakarta

> I am writing this poem
> >about the 1965 massacre
> >of Indonesians by Indonesians
>
> which in an article ten years later
> >I could not publish
> >except in Nottingham England with
>
> a friend Malcolm Caldwell who has since
> >himself been murdered
> >no one will say by whom but I will guess
>
> seeing as this is
> >precisely poetry

In the political world, as Peter Dale Scott implies in these lines, poetry is invisible. In the poetry world, political poetry is mostly preaching to the converted, making one want—almost too frequently—to quote Yeats: "Rhetoric comes out of a quarrel with others, poetry out of a quarrel with ourselves." Of course, the conditions are not propitious. We live behind vast screens of "information" and jargon, making even the most disastrous public events seem, as Peter Scott writes, like a "silent avalanche" seen from across a valley. If we are upper-middle-class, we rarely see those who pay the price for our prosperity, at home or elsewhere. We know our politicians do not debate the issues as they really are; and the polls tell us who will win months before we cast our tiny votes. We have

Agni 31/32 (1990).

very little sense of power, but just enough—to quote Scott again—"to feel guilty."

Coming to Jakarta tries to attack the problem from both ends, using poetry to smuggle in public truths undiscussed elsewhere, and at the same time writing out of that "quarrel with ourselves" that arises when we look at our political behavior honestly, in the full context of our lives and values. The two goals might seem almost incompatible; and it takes a long poem almost as intricate and digressive as Pound's *Cantos* to pull them together. But the result seems to me one of the three or four books of the last ten years that make "political poetry" something more than a cheering section for various fashionable causes.

On the public, or educative, side, Scott is concerned with what narrow circles of extreme power sometimes lie behind the vast blank of "information." Specifically, that "massacre / of Indonesians by Indonesians," when the army overthrew Sukarno and suppressed the Communist Party, and more than half a million people were killed. Painstakingly, with side notes and a bibliography, Scott documents how it was planned and financed by the CIA, oil companies, Lockheed, the Ford Foundation, and even Scott's (and my) own employer, the University of California. The more and less willing distortion of such events by the media, and by academic jargon, is a part of Scott's subject. Another part is the surreal politics of double bluff and disinformation in our age: how, some years later in Chile, the warning *Djakarta se acerca* (from which Scott takes his title) was sent by provocateurs to both sides, to drive both into extreme actions and precipitate the coup against Allende. Yet another part is the subtle forms political harrassment can take in a supposedly "open" society:

> the time when Paul's voice
>
> though just ten blocks away
> > was like a phone call from Minsk
> > I said *give us our sound back please*
>
> and the burst of volume
> > sent my ear reeling
> > Even the lawyer

for the House Select Committee
            said *I've never heard*
            noises like that on a telephone before

and he never phoned back
            so I can't blame you Gore
            that after the fourth disconnection

I never got the chance
            to proceed with my sentence

In such a situation, individual guilt and complicity are as
hard to measure as to deny. How guilty are the interlocutors
who are not "blame[d]" in the preceding passage? How guilty
is the eminent sociologist, who chooses to explain the massa-
cre in terms of native traditions of violence—the Balinese
cockfight, the trance drama—and to whom Scott says, "some-
times / the world is not as mysterious / as you and I might
wish?" How guilty are Scott and I, for continuing to adorn the
"front window / of the world's largest weapons lab"?

But the poem is not really concerned with adjudicating
degrees of guilt—rather, with casting a novelist's cold eye on
the nuances of political behavior. One of its best-known pas-
sages has to do with an early experience of civil disobedience
in the Free Speech movement at Berkeley:

we were thirty faculty
            asserting a high view
            of our constitutional rights

and when the patrolmen
            arms linked billy-clubs
            presented but not menacing

began to push us
            so silently you could still hear
            the baffled pigeons

the fountain in the wet gloom
            they came first to myself
            and to David Krech

who had already suffered
            his first bad heart attack
            I looked in his face

> forgetting all the others
> as if to say *Krech*
> *what does one do now*

Such a reaction must have been hard to admit to in print. (No wonder, Scott reflects, "there / is no easier task / than to sweep away faculty.") But for the reader, it carries the sense of discovery of truly new subject matter. Why, one wonders, did we ever want political poetry to be a poetry of *opinions?* When our *behavior* as political animals is so much more interesting, and less likely to appear in the newspapers.

Scott, it is true, is in a peculiarly privileged position to write about political behavior. Berkeley in the 1960s is to some degree common property, though rarely written about so calmly and well. But Scott has also lived near the pinnacles of extreme power. His father was a prominent Canadian Socialist; but the family vacationed at a lake on the border whose American side was "of a compact so invisible / and seamless as to exclude mere wealth." One of the most unnerving aspects of his Indonesian researches is the discovery that he actually knows some of the principal plotters, or their close relatives. His portrait of the wracked nerves, generational struggles, and religious obsessions of the Dulles clan has a human seriousness that bears comparison with Lowell's famous stanza on Lyndon Johnson. But Scott himself, as a young Canadian diplomat, has seen the world a little from their side—the insecurity, clubbiness, the "Mission code machines," limousines sent at midnight, the unconscious pleasure of enforcing restrictions—a subtle *descensus averni,* the "unique degradations / which follow upon any / categorical assumption // of command."

But the merits of this poem go beyond even its immense, indeed epic, range of political experience. Scott says he aspires to an "integrative poetry"—an almost impossible aspiration, it would seem. Our lives of thought, religion, Eros, self-definition are lived, to use Orwell's metaphor, inside the whale. We cannot separate our class position from the affections of a lifetime. Radical poets routinely attack the domestic ones for assuming their pleasures and values are "apolitical"; but surely they are no more hypocritical than the radicals

themselves, apologizing in their art for a civility they take for
granted in daily life. It is a two-faced Gorgon few of us can
look at and live. Yet that is exactly what Scott asks us to do:

> A poem of water
> > why not the mountains
> > the freedom on summits
>
> to come down any side
> > even the familiar one
> > these afternoons I
>
> walk up past the Rad Lab
> > to look west from Grizzly Peak
> > above the dim mists
>
> in the skyscrapers
> > the boats going nowhere
> > and with dusk the first urgent
>
> flashes of the signal
> > taking over the night
> > from uninhabited Alcatraz

Every element in this scene is a sign of collective guilt and
danger; and every element quickens with a haiku-like plea-
sure in the physical world as it has been given to us in our one
place and time. The poet's mind is drawn back to his grati-
tude, as a child, to his parents for moving to a higher, wealth-
ier neighborhood and saving him from being bullied in the
streets. Inescapable, that gratitude; and inescapable too, per-
haps, the fantasies of ghosts that began then, when violence
was removed from the surface of the child's life.

Only connect, E. M. Forster said; and Scott's integrative poem
is such a tissue of connections that one sometimes feels they can
never stop, like intersecting ripples on a pond. He too takes up
the Balinese trance drama. At one point, it helps to refute the
crudities of a journalist who says the Communists

> *went to their deaths*
> *in white funeral robes*
> *with an astonishing passivity*
>
> *as if admitting their guilt*

But at another point, it helps Scott himself ritually remember the astonishing amount of violent suffering in his own "normal" family history. Ezra Pound, in so many ways the model for such a poem, becomes one of its subjects; and his anti-Semitism is handled, characteristically, not by rote denunciations, but by a detailed account of the real personalities and actions of his bêtes noires, the Rothschilds. Etc., etc.

There are, obviously, dangers to such a method for poetry. *Coming to Jakarta* gives even less sense of beginning-middle-and-end, or of why a particular section belongs in one place rather than another, than do *Paterson* and *The Cantos*. (It is, mercifully, much shorter.) When it comes time to conclude, the reader does panic a little, on Scott's behalf. Such tensions, such interlocking relevancies, seem as inconclusible as life itself; the very act of articulating them a kind of blind faith, that "*If you bring forth / what is within you / it will save you.*" And the few passages of advice (other than that one, which comes from the Gnostic Gospels) seem at once obviously true; rhetorical as the rest of the poem is not; and futile in their generality—

> *relax trust*
> *spend more time with your children*
>
> *things can only go*
> *a little better*
> *if you do not hang on so hard*

And yet, unlike *The Cantos, Coming to Jakarta* is almost hypnotically readable. There are at least two reasons for this. One is Scott's personality. Wry, conscientious, self-deprecating, he never casts himself in a heroic role. His gentleness makes him particularly good at dealing with anger; and this is a rare virtue indeed. Most American political poetry is so bad, when it gets angry, that one is tempted to forget Dante, Blake, and Milton and take the high line that poetry, being compassionate, *cannot* lose its temper. But really the problem may be considerably more local. In the 1960s, being intemperate became a kind of holy self-immolation, a way of proving one was not hiding under the cloak of "complexity," like Hubert Humphrey or the Trillings. "Revolution or death." "Now Johnson would go up to join the great simulacra of men, / Hitler and Stalin." The habit has died hard, in left-wing poetry. But actually, when intelligent, humane people get angry about politics, they are much more likely to sound the way Scott does, reproaching himself for having been too polite to a political scientist in a debate. What happened was this: after the student audience applauded Scott for saying *"you / political scientists // are part of the problem,"*

                              I

            hushed them and turned
                    to apologize *of course*
                not you personally

            I did not know then
                    you had publicly castigated
                old friends in

            the Indonesian military
                    for not *carrying out*
                a control function

            for lacking
                    the ruthlessness
                that made it possible

            for the Nazis to suppress
                    the Communist party
                a few weeks after the elections

            in which the Communist party
            won five million votes

This not only has the naturalness of voice Levertov and Duncan lack, it is simply good writing: the documentation, the understatement, the sarcastic quotation, the stinging pacing. And it is not even righteous, because Scott is accusing himself of a mistake.

Then, there is the matter of form. Scott has learned everything there is to learn from Williams's variable foot, about how a regular/irregular short-line form can simplify tortuous sentences and bring out the spoken energy of a proselike style. But even more, I am thinking of a narrative skill much more common among fiction writers than poets—a seemingly digressive development that suddenly pulls tight as a net around the reader and the subject. Since this seems to me, very largely, the key to the poem's success, I would like to devote my remaining space to showing how it works within a single subsection, III.viii. The section begins with a minor, but personally momentous, instance of political evil. Scott has just been "ploughed" (failed) on his graduate exams at Oxford, for apprenticing himself to an outsider don, Michael Foster, who takes Hegel too seriously for the local positivists:

> so there was no extra year
> > as editor of the *Isis*
> it was back to Canada
>
> and a small school
> > for the over-privileged
> in the woods of the Seignory Club
>
> where at night I read
> > about Yvain in the forest
> *com hon forsenez et sauvage*
>
> but after the weekly movies
> > the whole school cheering
> the gooks on Okinawa
>
> once more incinerated
> > in the jets of napalm spewed
> from the tanks of the Marines
>
> lights out the generator switched off
> > I would go out in the moonlight
> boots squeaking on snow
>
> to empty the steadily filling
> > buckets of maple sap
> into the boys' vats
>
> and stoke their banked fires
> > the woods' shadows numinous
> with sugary smoke

> and I have since believed
> >> in the face of
> >> every nuclear headline
>
> the force flooding those
> >> millions of high trees
> >> even in the frost of night
>
> will survive the next war
> >> whether or not we do
> >> and I found I had the courage
>
> to make my young warriors
> >> read one account
> >> of an actual lynching

Yvain might perhaps have been predicted—a retrospectively soothing light on the poet's situation; exile, the value of wildness, the fool who returns as a hero. But the climactic digression into lyricism, nature, and nuclear war—without ever saying *this is how bad I felt,* or *this is how basic, and biological, the powers of self-healing are*—and then the move, without even a stanza break, to the first slight evidence of the poet's own recovery: that took a kind of genius. A few lines later, the recovery has become sexual as well; and then there is the *coup de foudre* at the end:

> Three years later I went back
>
> on my honeymoon with Maylie
> >> to that tall carpeted room
> >> over Christ Church Meadow
>
> asking in effect
> >> from this same new-found power
> >> *How can you stand it here?*
>
> And Michael Foster a few months
> >> before he shot himself
> >> looked around at the oak
>
> panels from Cardinal Wolsey
> >> and said *I can't imagine*
> >> *any better life*

It is a kind of Jamesian hourglass: the brilliant teacher inexplicably destroyed at the very moment the helpless student finds himself at last on solid ground. And—again, quite unexplicitly—it counterbalances, sets a limit to the section's earlier promises of limitless healing: there is no "better life" in which evil will not destroy forces, or people, of incalculable value.

This kind of Möbius loop of narrative seems to me Scott's fundamental discovery as a worker in the long poem: what he adds to what he inherits from Pound and Williams. He does not try, any more than they did, to build from these moments of discovery, or clarified contradiction, a single overriding narrative arc. It may be a defining characteristic of the modern long poem to be a triumph of breadth of experience and repeating forms of local order—like fractals in mathematics—over the expectation of overarching order, a calculable relation of part to whole. If so, it seems peculiarly promising as a way of writing about politics, where general conclusions are difficult indeed. Triumph over the system has seemed, since the 1960s, almost unbelievable; and triumph in the direction of what other system is, in the days of perestroika, problematic. We do not want poems to be empty boasts; we do not want them to tell us to lie down and die, either. Immediate right action; small acts of unpopular truth-telling; a refusal to compartmentalize awareness, even though "we live by forgetting"—this is what Scott's poem asks of us, at its widest stretch. And without ever asking the unanswerable question, Yeats's question: "O when may it suffice?"

Poetry and Politics (II)

Almost everyone wants there to be political poetry—as if it were the badge of our seriousness, our membership in the greater human community. And almost no one, except for a few diehard activists, is satisfied with most of the political poetry we have. It is a subject one almost hesitates to write on at all, fearing one is bound to expose something bad—a cryptoconservatism, or wishy-washy quietism, if not some narrow-minded "political correctness." But the question nags. How many times do we hear quoted at us—always with respect, usually with some sense of guilt or shame—the Latin American poet's judgment about our "little personal poems"? (But would we really want our poetry to be like *their* second-string, at least as it appears in translation—those blunt newspaper cartoons, the good side all soft porn, young mothers nursing in the fields, the bad side all rape and jackboots?)

To give us the courage of our doubts, let us listen to another voice, out of the Stalinist experience of Eastern Europe, Milan Kundera's in *The Unbearable Lightness of Being*:

> What repelled her was not nearly so much the ugliness of the Communist world . . . as the mask of beauty it tried to wear—in other words, Communist kitsch. . . . The unwritten, unsung motto of the parade was not "Long live Communism!" but "Long live life!" The power and cunning of Communist politics lay in the fact that it appropriated this slogan. . . .
>
> The feeling induced by kitsch must be a kind the multitudes can share. Kitsch may not, therefore, depend on an unusual

situation; it must derive from the basic images people have engraved in their memories: the ungrateful daughter, the neglected father, children running on the grass, the motherland betrayed, first love.

Kitsch causes two tears to flow in quick succession. The first tear says: How nice to see children running on the grass!

The second tear says: How nice to be moved, together with all mankind, by children running on the grass!

It is the second tear that makes kitsch kitsch.

The brotherhood of man on earth will be possible only on a base of kitsch. . . .

Kitsch is the aesthetic ideal of all politicians and all political parties and movements.[1]

Do we hear some rather large pedestals starting to crack at these words? That "second tear," that tone of self-congratulation at being on the side of humanity, whether positively or negatively (for we congratulate ourselves on what we abhor, as well as on what moves us) is what some of us dislike in most political poetry, even when we agree with the message. Can there be a political art that does not rely on kitsch?

It might be fruitful to pose the question differently. What can poetry do with politics that a newspaper editorial, a cartoon, a speech cannot do as well, or better? One answer, I would suggest, is that it has a lot more leeway to deal with mixed feelings—with that ambivalence that may seem indecisive, even treacherous, in the moment, but is almost bound to have some merit in the long run, given the unexpected outcomes of human undertakings. It may be an ambivalence between elements of different political positions, as with Robert Lowell, who was quite sincerely conservative, liberal, and radical, according to his temperament and the differences between situations. It may be caused by a conflict (or simply an interaction) between a political position and other frameworks of value—personal loyalty, aesthetics, religion—that are equally real to the individual. Here, too, poetry may have a special advantage in examining those auras of aesthetic feeling that surround the political, and give it, legitimately or illegitimately, so much of its intrapsychic authority. Or poetry might deal with the sense of powerful drifts in one's own unconscious life, or in other people's, that impede one's freedom to act rationally for a common good. It can even articulate hatred, though, if it is as sensitive as we wish poetry to be, it will also articulate the pain of hatred as a state of mind. The poet is then implicated in the full texture, the confusions, and the guilt of human interaction, not raised above it in the false superiority of Kundera's kitsch.

I am suggesting, then, a poetry "including politics," in the sense in which Pound wanted the *Cantos* to be a "poem including history." What this leaves out, admittedly, are the situations in which poems get written because editorials would not be published, or would be suppressed—what Carolyn Forché calls "poetry of witness." While some poets of "witness" do use the broad, simple strokes of kitsch, others—one thinks of Celan and Bobrowski—have been as brilliant in the invention of new language as any Modernist, realizing that the language of editorials cannot make the experience of extremity real, to the reader who has not suffered it.

What I am *not* recommending, in any way, is "complexity" as a comfortable way of sitting on the sidelines. The political poems that move me most are the private thoughts of people capable of taking sides, taking strong action. But such poems, one hopes, may affect the criteria for action—making them more loyal to a morality of means, less likely to deny the adversary's human presence, than politics by itself often is.

I

Yeats is seldom mentioned in serious discussions of political poetry, Terrence Des Pres's *Praises and Dispraises* being the honorable exception. His values are too aristocratic, so that he's often dismissed with the generic prejudice that all male Modernists were crypto-fascists, anyway. Yet in some ways he had almost the ideal situation for a political poet. He lived at the heart of revolutionary times. He was an activist, so that he saw the gritty day-to-day meshing of personalities and circumstances ("the day's war with every knave and dolt, / Theater business, management of men") which is always the body of real politics, however ethereal or inspired its soul. And his own mixed feelings—because of Maud Gonne, because of Parnell, because of his own Anglo-Irish country squire background—were too tumultuous ever to let him rest in the ideological.

"Easter, 1916" is one of my favorite political poems, because it is an affirmative revolutionary poem, which nonetheless has ample room for other values, reflections, doubts. It is a poem of self-questioning from the very start, because—as is well known—it is a recantation of another poem. In "September 1913," Yeats had dismissed the Irish Catholic middle class as too puritanical, too avaricious, ever to be "Romantic" or heroic again. Now, that class had produced some of the heroes of the Easter Rebellion.

I don't think all readers realize just how savage a story Yeats is telling on himself in the opening lines of "Easter, 1916":

> I have met them at close of day
> Coming with vivid faces
> From counter or desk among grey
> Eighteenth-century houses.
> I have passed with a nod of the head
> Or polite meaningless words,
> Or have lingered awhile and said
> Polite meaningless words,
> And thought before I had done
> Of a mocking tale or a gibe
> To please a companion
> Around the fire at the club.

Face to face with the future heroes, Yeats has relieved his boredom by turning their behavior into funny stories, with which he will later "please" an upper-class, presumably conservative, "companion." (Professor J. V. Kelleher at Harvard insisted that "the club" was a recognizable, Anglo-Irish one, which the heroes could not have entered, because they were Catholics.) What a contrast to the self-righteousness, the automatic identification with the good side, in most political poetry! Having confessed his disreputable behavior, Yeats goes

on to make an issue of the attitudes that made it possible—
worldly cynicism, the conviction that since he lived in a world
of comedy ("Being certain that they and I / But lived where
motley is worn"), irony, proportion, the "Eighteenth-century"
values "the club" could accept, were what qualified one as
civilized, as fully human.

These values, it is important to say, are not simply wrong;
they have been "changed," by the hidden potential the heroes
have revealed. The comic world has become the tragic one—
the world of "terrible beauty," which, as all readers of Nietz-
sche know, is what the *sparagmos,* the tearing apart of Diony-
sus, adds to Apollo's vision of eternal symmetry. I think of the
paradoxical relief that some of us, veterans of the 1960s, felt
seeing LA flare up on television—the relief of living again in
tragic times, when people would actually stake everything on
a sense of justice. For Yeats, as for us, it is partly a moral
relief—the relief of being encouraged to live from a larger
conception of ourselves.

And yet, before glorifying the heroes, Yeats cannot resist
telling us what they were like, how he judged them, in "the
casual comedy." Constance Gore-Booth had had a natural
grace and rightness as an aristocratic young horsewoman; as
an activist she was "ignorant," "shrill," given over, in Jung's
terms, to a hostile and rationalizing animus. MacBride, Maud
Gonne's husband, is of course "A drunken, vainglorious lout."
Pearse is generally thought to come off better, but listen to the
lines:

> This man had kept a school
> And rode our wingèd horse.

A great poet does not use a dead metaphor for no reason, or
add an archaizing accent mark, to show that a word must be
mispronounced for the meter. Yeats is telling us—those who
have ears to hear—what he thought of Pearse's poetry, and
perhaps of any poetry that is too much "our(s)," too ready to
set nationalism, the collective, ahead of individual tempera-
ment. Only MacDonagh really comes out unscathed, and he
because of what he "might have" become, not what he was.

The problem, then, for Yeats is to come to terms with what he has resisted in the heroes, which is also what made possible their action: their singleness of vision. It has set them apart, in a magic realm; it has also hardened them.

> Hearts with one purpose alone
> Through summer and winter seem
> Enchanted to a stone
> To trouble the living stream.

Terrence Des Pres sees the stone as a "near-miracle," like Kant's sublime, challenging the "humdrum stream of Heraclitean flux."[2] But this, I think, is to ignore the immense descriptive beauty lavished on the stream scene, a beauty which is unique in the poem, and which surely would not be wasted on a "humdrum" world, a world without significant claims:

> A shadow of cloud on the stream
> Changes minute by minute;
> A horse-hoof slides on the brim,
> And a horse plashes within it;
> The long-legged moor-hens dive,
> And hens to moor-cocks call;
> Minute by minute they live:
> The stone's in the midst of all.

The imagery recalls Yeats's preference for Constance Gore-Booth as a young horsewoman. It invokes the aristocratic world, and Yeats's abiding loyalty to what that world includes and the political one cannot: the aesthetic pure and simple, a Zen-like alertness to the changes of the moment, a love of multitudinous, rich, and erotic instability.

The elegy, then, is partly an elegy for what people lose when they see life as exclusively political—their sense of humor, their aestheticism, even the more individual forms of compassion. In case we have missed the usual implication of conjoining "stone" and "heart," Yeats spells it out for us:

> Too long a sacrifice
> Can make a stone of the heart.

In another poem, placed near this one in the *Collected Poems*, Yeats catches the "heart"-failings of radicals with a precision no honest campaigner from the 1960s can fail to recognize:

> They must to keep their certainty accuse
> All that are different of a base intent;
> Pull down established honour; hawk for news
> Whatever their loose fantasy invent
> And murmur it with bated breath, as though
> The abounding gutter had been Helicon
> Or calumny a song.

But in "Easter, 1916" the fools have become heroes, and so even the judgment is compassionate: they have hardened, not because of evil nature, but because of too much defeat and disappointment, "Too long a sacrifice." So that the following question, "O when may it suffice," is addressed not to the radicals, but to the dark Providence that has tried their merely human virtues so severely. And even this question is left to "Heaven." "[O]ur part" is—as Des Pres has pointed out—a bardic and traditional naming, a summoning up of the maternal soul of the race to sing the heroes to sleep, to free them, as Rilke would have put it, from "the appearance of suffered injustice":

> To murmur name upon name,
> As a mother names her child
> When sleep at last has come
> On limbs that had run wild.

Though even here, there is a world of tender ambivalence, toward the self and toward the heroes, in the image that presents the poet as at once mature and feminine, his subjects as male, "wild"—but children. The sadder maternal wisdom has a political dimension as well. Perhaps it was "needless death"; perhaps the path of negotiated compromise would have worked:

> For England may keep faith
> For all that is done and said.

It is the last test of rigorous honesty in the poem—one no speechwriter could ever pass. But really, it is invoked only to be swept aside. For by now the poem has resolved its quarrel between aesthetics and purposefulness through the deep aesthetics of politics: how a grand enough image, however impractical, can make a nation, where before there was only the congeries of "motley" self-interests, judgments, ironies.

> MacDonagh and MacBride
> And Connolly and Pearse
> Now and in time to be,
> Wherever green is worn,
> Are changed, changed utterly:
> A terrible beauty is born.

Contemporary readers might have some difficulty with this resolution on the aesthetic. For us, "image" is something consciously created and manipulated, so that the very word—as antonym to "substance"—produces a kind of political nausea. We want our poetry, and our criticism, to record that nausea, to take us behind the scenes and show us the manipulators at their work. But we did not always feel this way. Those of us who grew up under Kennedy know how much the power of the image surpassed the failings, and even the politics, of the man; and how much energy it released into the culture. Yeats reminds us that such collective energies, expressed in images, are not predictable, not containable by their manipulators; that they can work for good; and that they are always "terrible," always a little to be feared. In arguing the case on this level, he does something that poetry can do, and the editorial cannot. It can inhabit an exploratory middle ground between Realpolitik and the kind of emotional appeal always stigmatized as "blind."

II

Technology. The word itself, even in freshman essays, seems to carry an automatic freight of disapproval—a disapproval justified, God knows, by the thousand daily threats our luxuries pose to our survival. And yet, how many of us—even those who became the most abstruse intellectuals—have as children pored over a diagram of an internal combustion engine, or stood on a railway platform to watch the engine and its noise enlarge, from a minuscule chuffing dot at the horizon . . .

C. K. Williams's "Tar" is a complex poem about a technological disaster that must have occasioned many simplistic ones—Three Mile Island. Like many good political poems, it starts with something personal and apparently at the periphery, the "unusual situation" Kundera opposes to "kitsch."

> All morning a crew of workmen have been tearing the old
>   decrepit roof off our building,
> and all morning, trying to distract myself, I've been
>   wandering out to watch them
> as they hack away the leaden layers of asbestos paper and
>   disassemble the disintegrating drains.
> After half a night of listening to the news, wondering
>   how to know a hundred miles downwind
> if and when to make a run for it and where, then a coming
>   bolt awake at seven
> when the roofers we've been waiting for since winter sent
>   their ladders shrieking up our wall

The importance of the roofers will enlarge and enlarge through the poem. They bring in, first the theme of denial: all the small, half-conscious avoidances that have led people, in how many contexts, to ignore immense dangers, if only those dangers were intangible and far away. There is the impulse to "distract [one]self"; and the sheer inertia, the inconvenience of daily life, that make it a luxury to pay attention to anything more remote. (Workers in the construction trades are famous for arriving unannounced, as well as for months of unexplained delays.) There are also the nearer perils ("leaden layers of asbestos paper") that we live with daily, out of mere ignorance.

But just as important, I think, is the growing fascination the roofers' work exerts on the speaker, and the Whitmanesque evocative cataloging it provokes—so suited to Williams's long line. "The ladders flex and quiver, things skid from the edge," in a dazzle of colliding consonants, bouncing off each other like freight cars.

> Even the battered little furnace, roaring along as
>   patient as a donkey, chokes and clogs,
> a dense, malignant smoke shoots up, and someone has
>   to fiddle with a cock, then hammer it,
> before the gush and stench will deintensify, the dark,
>   Dantean broth wearily subside.
> In its crucible, the stuff looks bland, like licorice,
>   spill it, though, on your boots or coveralls,
> it sears, and everything is permeated with it, the furnace
>   gunked with burst and half-burst bubbles,
> the men themselves so completely slashed and mucked they
>   seem almost from another realm, like trolls.
> When they take their break, they leave their brooms
>   standing at attention in the asphalt pails,
> work gloves clinging like Brer Rabbit to the bitten shafts,
>   and they slouch along the precipitous lip,
> the enormous sky behind them, the heavy noontime air
>   alive with shimmers and mirages.

Of course, the details of this "matter-of-factly and harrowingly dangerous" work keep turning into metaphors for the disaster in the background. The "bland" tar "sears," and "permeate(s)" everything, once it spills. When something goes wrong with the engine, it is unexpectedly hard to fix, and the result is somehow infernal, "malignant smoke," a "dark, Dantean broth." The men move on the "precipitous lip" of the sky, and we cannot tell whether the "shimmers and mirages" of "noontime" come from the warmth of spring, from thousands of little engines like theirs, or from radiation.

And yet, how much fun Williams has finding verbal equivalents for all this explosive stickiness: "gunked," "permeated," "burst," "slashed and mucked." How wonderful the similes are, animate and homely just where we would expect them to be mechanistic and grim—the "little furnace . . . as patient as a donkey," the "work gloves clinging like Brer Rabbit to the bitten shafts." The little boy watching for the train is fully alive in the mature poet.

My point is that, as with Yeats, we have an abnegation of the usual moral authority of the political poet. As Williams implicates himself in collective denial, so too he involves himself, his ordinary American roofers, and the reader in the delights of playing with muck and matter which are the root of Three Mile Island. A mysterious, and deeply human, ambivalence toward our Faustian undertakings has entered in. We can no longer regard them innocently, as something foisted on us by a distant, criminally callous "they."

And yet, Williams pulls none of the punches we would expect in a more conventional protest poem. He can even, perhaps, carry off a scornful and dismissive tone more successfully, because his voice has so many other trustworthy registers. "[T]he slick federal spokesmen still have their evasions in some semblance of order." "I remember the president in his absurd protective booties, looking absolutely unafraid, the fool." (Here we face the large, but delicate, question of how anger is best expressed in political poems. There is no one answer, that fits all situations. But how much better the domestic, exasperated tone of "the fool" is—as well as fairer to Jimmy Carter's actual character—than any shriller denunciation! And how the little detail of the "protective booties" nails it down.) In the end, the poem rises to a judgment so prophetic and unequivocal that, reading it aloud to classes, I've had the impulse (which no more radical poem has ever given me) to stop then and there. If this is true, how can we be talking about *poetry?*

> we were going to perish of all this, if not now, then
> soon, if not soon, then someday.
> Someday, some final generation, hysterically aswarm
> beneath an atmosphere as unrelenting as rock,
> would rue us all, anathematize our earthly comforts,
> curse our surfeits and submissions.

But, of course, the poem itself doesn't stop here. It goes on:

> I think I know, though I might rather not, why my
> roofers stay so clear to me and why the rest,
> the terror of that time, the reflexive disbelief and
> distancing, all we should hold on to, dims so.

What the poet would "rather not" know, I would guess, is how involuntary denial is, how it goes on working—even in the shape of memory—when we know everything about how it works, and what the truth is, that we should cling to and act on, whether by flight, or by a lifetime of protest. (And the reader, too, is involved in this denial, simply by continuing to read the poem as a "poem.") Of course, one could take a more compassionate view of how memory operates in such situations, a view put forward by the psychoanalyst Christopher Bollas. Objects, Bollas says, can serve the "conservative" function of holding on to "preserved self states that prevailed in a child's life when he could not comprehend a nonetheless self-defining experience," presumably because its causes were too large, too pervasive, too traumatic. Like traumatic memories, these objects "stor[e]" something, in a disguised form, "for understanding in the future." Bollas gives an example from his own childhood:

> Very much in love before the war, my parents found themselves bewilderingly distanced after their reuniting and a mood of sad vexation pervaded the house for some time. As part of this scene I am sure that I knew something, but I did not have the means of thinking what I knew. . . . However, at my school I think I nominated an object—a swing—to conserve some aspects of this self state. I don't know why exactly, but I imagine that this thing which had been so much fun (it is an object for a joyful two-person relation), now empty and unoccupied, signified the absence of such pleasure.[3]

Williams's roofers can be seen as such a "mnemic object." For they have, in fact, preserved "the terror of that time, the reflexive disbelief and distancing," in a form that could issue in a poem, not an editorial. And they have shaped a future "understanding" which is complex, involving basic human motives and collective complicity. Whether such aesthetic recovery is an adequate response is, of course, another question—one the poem itself addresses, obliquely and symbolically, at the end:

> Even the leftover carats of tar in the gutter, so black
>   they seemed to suck the light out of the air.
> By nightfall kids had come across them: every sidewalk
>   on the block was scribbled with obscenities and hearts.

Will the human race survive because of its daily inventiveness, or perish because of its daily denial? Especially when the inventiveness expresses all sides of our nature, "obscenities and hearts." The prophecy pulls toward one answer, as does the light "suck[ed] . . . out of the air"; the mildly upbeat tone of the last line pulls toward another. We are left—as we *are* left—in the middle.

These poems—and one could of course adduce others—neither separate the "personal" from the "political," nor politicize the personal in order to push it toward one monolithic interpretation; rather, they set the political in the fuller context of being human. Whether the reader finds them as deeply satisfying as I do will depend, largely, on what he or she wants from poetry. If one wants a rallying cry or a marching song, Williams's poem is much too defeatist, and even Yeats's too qualified. If one wants historical or sociological information, the kind of information from which the middle-class reader is likely to be sheltered, then Forché's "witness" is an honorable other tradition. But if one thinks of poetry as its own very special kind of knowledge, moving between different areas of consciousness as it moves between the abstract principle and the individual case—then one will be grateful for the kinds of information more argumentative media cannot bring. For auras, ambivalences, unconscious drifts; for Yeats's sense both of the limitations of the political life and the transforming power of its images; for Williams's sense of how complexly our inventiveness and our cowardice, together, are hurtling us toward the unknown future.

Notes

1. Milan Kundera, *The Unbearable Lightness of Being,* trans. Michael Henry Heim (New York: Harper Colophon Books, 1985), 248–51.

2. Terrence Des Pres, *Praises & Dispraises* (New York: Viking Penguin, 1988), 60.

3. Christopher Bollas, *Being a Character* (New York: Hill and Wang, 1992), 19–20.

The Values of Contemporary
European Poetry

I

My title should perhaps be more modest: *some* values of *some*
contemporary European poets. In writing about European po-
etry at all, I am very much aware of conducting my education
in public. But I wish to pinpoint a certain kind of stance—
especially toward civilization and history—which more and
more seems to me characteristic, and wise, and valuably differ-
ent from that of most American poetry I read. Contemporary
European poets have absorbed, often by brutal necessity, the
shocks of the twentieth century; yet they know that if life is to
be affirmed at all, it must be one's own life, in one's own time,
out of one's own particular traditions. They do not divide, as
American writers so often and notoriously do, into "palefaces"
and "redskins": on the one hand, a primitivism which (despite
heroic exceptions like Gary Snyder) is often escapist, anti-
cultural, anti-intellectual; on the other, an urbane, this-worldly
poetry too little able to take account of how drastically this
world has changed, and goes on changing. The European po-
ets cherish, and use, the immense repository of values, insights,
joys, that we all carry with us from the civilized past; yet the
primitive ground beneath civilization, and the apocalyptic pos-
sibilities awaiting it, are always near at hand.

By the same token, the best European poetry does not divide
the personality into a daylight self and an unconscious or

American Poetry Review 13, no. 1 (January–February 1984).

dream self, presumed to be outside history. Those who have only read American writings about European poetry may be surprised by this statement; American poets have had reason to admire the Europeans for plunging fearlessly into an unconscious or associative dimension. But what is finally most remarkable is the way in which this dimension is integrated with the quotidian, and with the reflective or philosophical.

For the positive values in contemporary European poetry—and for a sense of how the civilized and the primitive are held in balance—I can hardly do better than to turn to the great recent poem "Schubertiana," by the Swedish poet Tomas Tranströmer.[1] The poem begins with a vision of modern agglomeration (New York City seen from an "outlook point") as eerily enormous, out of control: "a long shimmering drift, a spiral galaxy seen from the side." Incessant stimulus locks horns there with incessant fear: "behind doors with police locks a perpetual seethe of voices." Yet still, a cultural artifact can displace all this, bringing an individual life to a single point of focus:

> I know too—without statistics—that right now Schubert
> is being played in some room over there and that for
> someone the notes are more real than all the rest.

The choice of music as the vehicle of transcendence might, in an American context, already range the writer in the "paleface" camp. But things are not so simple here. For what is at issue is not so much Art, with a capital *A*, as the whole encoding, condensing, symbol-making faculty of the human brain—and of the animal brain before it—as the brilliant second section of the poem makes clear:

> The endless expanses of the human brain are crumpled to
> the size of a fist.
> In April the swallow returns to last year's nest under
> the guttering of this very barn in this very parish.
> She flies from Transvaal, passes the equator, flies for
> six weeks over two continents, makes for precisely
> this vanishing dot in the land-mass.
> And the man who catches the signals from a whole life
> in a few ordinary chords for five strings,

who makes a river flow through the eye of a needle,
is a stout young gentleman from Vienna known to his
    friends as "The Mushroom" who slept with his glasses on
and stood at his writing desk punctually of a morning.
And then the wonderful centipedes of his manuscript
    were set in motion.

Many things here—besides the swallow, and the anatomical view of the brain—serve to generalize our sense of the creative process. For one thing, Schubert is much less of a special case than we usually like the artist to be; he is not dashing, not free of bourgeois inhibition or orderliness. (Perhaps it is partly this sense of the distance between the music and Schubert's surface personality that leads Robert Bly, in the introduction to his fine translation of *Truth Barriers,* to see the poem's vision of music as wholly transcendental: "pure sound vibrations connected apparently to feelings (but not to experiences) that resonate somewhere inside us. . . . a layer of consciousness that runs alongside our life, above or below, but is not it."[2] But I would argue that it is precisely Tranströmer's refusal to divide up consciousness in this way—his emphasis instead on condensed experience, "the signals from a whole life"—that differentiates him from American poets who share his interest in the mysterious, the more-than-rational.)

Finally, we notice how Tranströmer dwells on the artisanal or technological side of music: the "wonderful centipedes" of musical notation, "the eye of a needle" which is surely the modern phonograph needle as well as Schubert's pen. As Tranströmer does not absolutely distinguish human from animal intelligence, so he does not separate the ingenuity of the encoding mechanism from the beauty or intricacy of what is encoded, in his feeling of "wonder." His subject becomes, in the most inclusive sense, mind, responding to and organizing the world.

Perhaps this is a good place to digress on what is probably the most salient, or novel, feature of Tranströmer's style: the mingling of the organic and the scientific or technological, and especially the introduction of technological metaphors into the most sacrosanct preserves of high poetry—nature, art, the preindustrial past. These comparisons are almost always illuminating, and, because they are so unexpected, freshening. "The crickets whirr their sewing-machines frantically"; "the lonely water-tap rises among the wild roses / like the statue of a horseman"; "I pause with my hand on the door-handle, take the pulse of the house";

> Out on the sun-warmed lichens the insects scurry,
>   they're in a rush like second-hands—the pine
>   throws a shadow, it migrates gently like an
>   hour-hand—.

These examples are taken from a few pages of the long poem "Baltics"; but similar ones could be found almost anywhere in Tranströmer's work. Beyond the pleasure of novelty, they move us, I think, because they accept—as so little poetry does—the fact that a man-made world constitutes the norm for us, without reflection, without satire, most of the time. But conversely, the same metaphors remind us that our world is not absolute; that it grows out of, and serves, preexisting biological needs. A house that has a pulse is not so remote from the snail's "house" we hear of a few lines later. Seaweed—again in "Baltics"—"holds itself up with air-bladders as we hold ourselves up with ideas."

At the same time, what it means to hold oneself up—the purpose, or the satisfaction, of merely being—remains as mysterious for a man as for a seaweed. And I think this is what "Schubertiana" is finally getting at through the metaphor of music. At any rate, another of Tranströmer's very striking mechanical comparisons—for a four-hand piano piece—suggests as much:

> The hands seem to be moving resonant weights to and fro,
>   as if we were tampering with the counterweights
> in an effort to disturb the great scale arm's terrible
>   balance: joy and suffering weighing exactly the same.

On the one hand, music disturbs the balance by restoring to us an undefended inchoacy, an infantile playfulness toward a still half-fluid universe:

> The string quintet is playing. I walk home through warm
>   forests with the ground springy under me,
> curl up like an embryo, fall asleep, roll weightless into
>   the future.

On the other hand, music can suggest the active, almost religious, confidence that allows us to project ourselves, with our weight, into that same future, in spite of the odds. This is the subject of the most moving single section of the poem, the fourth, which I quote in its entirety:

> So much we have to trust, simply to live through our daily
>   day without sinking into the earth!
> Trust the piled snow clinging to the mountain slope above the
>   village.
> Trust the promises of silence and the smile of under-
>   standing, trust that the accident telegram isn't for us and
>   that the sudden axe-blow from within won't come.
> Trust the axles that carry us on the highway in the middle of
>   the three hundred times life-size bee-swarm of steel.
> But none of that is really worth our confidence.
> The five strings say we can trust something else. What else?
>   Something else, and they keep us company part of the way
>   there.
> As when the time-switch clicks off in the stairwell and the
>   fingers—trustingly—follow the blind handrail that finds
>   its way in the darkness.

At the end of the poem, music (with its accumulated meanings, active trust and delighted play) seems to become a metaphor for identity—for the self, or the energy, that remains constant, and elucidates itself, through all the moods and activities of life:

> The long melody that remains itself in all
>   its transformations, sometimes glittering and pliant,
>   sometimes rugged and strong, snail-track and steel
>   wire.
> The perpetual humming that follows us—now—
> up
> the depths.

It is a kind of religion of art, if one likes; but art, by now, so inclusively defined that it is impossible to imagine "life" as an opposing term.

And yet, like the traditional religion-of-art poem, "Schubertiana" includes an attack on the philistines—albeit a different sort of philistine than would have preoccupied Arnold or Baudelaire. Immediately preceding the concluding lines I have just quoted, one finds this passage:

> Annie said, "This music is so heroic," and she's right.
> But those whose eyes enviously follow men of action, who
>   secretly despise themselves for not being murderers, don't
>   recognize themselves here,
> and the many who buy and sell people and believe that
>   everyone can be bought, don't recognize themselves here,
> not their music.

The philistines, here, are not those who hate art (perhaps some music *is* their music), but those who would reduce life to struggle and function, and heroism to Darwinian success—ignoring the "long melody" of being's inner delight in itself, both active and contemplative. On first reading, I must say that the scolding, moralistic tone of these lines bothered me; and to some degree it still does. (Though possibly my discomfort stems partly from the neatness with which the lines reduce to absurdity a kind of self-hatred not uncommon among intellectuals.) Yet it now seems to me that the lines bring forth an ethical criterion wholly congruent with all the thought and feeling in the poem. The poem's many and subtle definitions, through music, of the courage and creativity involved in mere conscious being, allow the concept of the "heroic" to be transferred from the realm of violence to that being—to ordinary decency, sensitivity, and endurance.

As one might expect from this, when Tranströmer's poetry touches on actual politics, it is humane, psychologically acute, many-sided, and unideological. "From an African Diary (1963)"—a subject most white Western writers would probably find too ticklish to begin with—shows the same kind of understanding of mixed motives, and the shame and confusion that result from them, that we find in Forster's *A Passage to India:*

> A young African found a tourist lost among the huts.
> He couldn't decide whether to make him a friend or
>   object of blackmail.
> The indecision upset him. They parted in confusion.[3]

Tranströmer acknowledges the corruption and waste often seen in emerging countries—

> The student studies all night, studies and studies so
>   he can be free.
> When the examination is over, he turns into a stair-rung
>   for the next man.

—without either denying the Africans' idealism or casting all the blame back onto the colonial period. (Though Europeans are not exactly treated indulgently: they "huddle around their cars as if the cars were Mama.") Rather, the emphasis is on "human energy saddened" by the enormity of the problems, and the internal clash between two cultures. As the refrain lines put it,

> The road from one way of life to another is hard.
> Those who are ahead have a long way to go.

When Tranströmer tries to imagine what "would help," his lines take on the whimsy of desperation:

> Perhaps a migratory flock of handshakes would help.
> Perhaps letting the truth escape from books would help.
> We have to go farther.

Yet the variation on the refrain line here is important, and moving. I can imagine a Marxist reader dismissing it as unreal liberal good will; for me it has force because it involves everyone—the poet, as well as the Africans—in an unequal but very real struggle between good will and the inertia of historical roles. But then, Tranströmer is a liberal, in the least complacent sense of the word; and has suffered, I understand, in Swedish literary politics for not being more of a leftist. In the closest thing to a political manifesto I have seen in his work, he writes:

> Radical and Reactionary live together as in an
>   unhappy marriage,
> moulded by one another, dependent on one another.
> But we who are their children must break loose.
> Every problem cries in its own language.[4]

In this attitude, Tranströmer is typical of the best contemporary European poetry—in marked contrast to other areas of creative endeavor, notably Deconstruction, where a strong element in the intellectual mix is still the reactive, *épater le bourgeois* strain of cultural radicalism which Tranströmer analyzes here with his characteristically pungent metaphorical irony.

II

One way to avoid being either radical or reactionary is to remember that, as Eliot said, "History has many cunning passages, contrived corridors": that defeat is not necessarily obliteration, any more than triumph is a guarantee of moral or cultural accomplishment. What is valuable can survive by devious pathways, even improve in the overlay of cultures. In a brilliant and provocative remark in the introduction to their valuable anthology *Another Republic*, Charles Simic and Mark Strand suggest that Cavafy is "the great modern ancestor" of the contemporary European poetry of history, "since he understood perhaps better than any of his contemporaries that in history nothing changes except the names, that there are always victims, always oppressors."[5] I think this insight could be carried still further. It is not only Cavafy's political disillusionment that is prototypical, but his great metaphor of Alexandria. The decadent city—which, itself powerless, survives to swallow Hellenism and empire, Gnosticism and Christianity—is in Cavafy not only the repository of wisdom but its emblem, scaling down to human size the too many superhuman claims of history. Alexandrias of various descriptions—fertile opposites to the city of God, of national or religious confidence—have haunted European poetry since the Second World War.

One of the most interesting instances is the Serbian poet Miodrag Pavlović, though he does not appear in *Another Republic,* and his work is, unfortunately, hard to find in English.[6] Living under a Marxism that, despite its liberal tinge, retains much of the cultural narrowness of a state religion, Pavlović takes as his subject all the strains of culture and belief that have gone under, yet somehow persisted, in Yugoslavian history: classical Hellenism; barbarian animism; the Bogomils, the persecuted eastern Cathars of the Middle Ages; and finally Serbian Christianity itself, in its last stand against the Turks at Smederevo. As Pavlović assumes the voice of each of these defeated factions in turn, in the book entitled *The Voice under the Stone,* we get a sense of suspended judgment and cumulative richness akin to Cavafy's—as we do, indeed, from the stance of many of the individual poems. Writing about "The Slavs before Parnassus"—barbarians, but also victims, demolishing the remains of classical Greece at the command of unnamed "leaders"—Pavlović avoids either celebrating the energy of savagery or lamenting the fall of civilization. Instead, through the voice of the bard, of "secret," dissident wisdom, he emphasizes the unexpected continuities and couplings of cultures:

> The singers asked us in secret
> who had attended the burial of heaven
> and who had witnessed the death-rattle of eternity.

> They still said: night should be filled
> with singing not destruction.

At the end of the poem, the singers envision a new transmission, or new fusion, between energy and the cultural ideal:

> the divine shape will appear with the dawn
> and hands shall rest upon our shoulders
> adopting us as new sons

> Our nakedness will then don words
> like the birchtree donning leaves in spring.

It is, of course, no accident that the poets are the carriers of this mixture of skepticism and profound, though doctrineless, faith. Poetry has always been more capable than politics or religion of conceding a deep experience of value to each of two conflicting principles or camps. But beyond that, the material of poetry, language itself, is for Pavlović the final repository of cultures—the level at which no once living component can be wholly refuted or excluded. Secure on this ground, Pavlović's "Old Slavic Bard"—like Yeats's Oisin—can even face the possible fact of a Christian Last Judgment:

> I'll stay where I am
> in the soil of my language,
> I don't want your councils to judge me;
> throw me beneath the open skies
> upon the cold grill of eternity.
> Let others appear before God,
> my hole is good enough for me:
> ancient words warm me like fleece,
> guzlas beneath the earth
> are made fertile by memory.

In another poem, "Svetovid"—a barbarian god, now "a nightmare" to the Christianized psyche—consoles himself in the same way:

> Bitter is the fate of the gods
> and bitterly we depend on the human species
> who changes both smell and faith at once.
>
> Only the beekeepers remain,
> cultivating honey in the trunks of language.

Against the history of the Balkans which yields these grim but resilient lessons, there stands always, in *The Voice under the Stone,* an image of the opposing principle, the city of God, which, for a man of the East, is of course not Rome but Constantinople. It is a deeply ambivalent image. The city is at once an intimidating adversary—the center of bureaucracy and worldliness, the triumph of the letter over the spirit—and the ideal polis, the gathering place of the whole life of the mind.

115

The envoy from Constantinople is unjustly and automatically preferred to the local saint; the pilgrim is ignored and shunted aside there, only to say in old age:

> I know that in that distant hour
> when I wandered alone and poor
> through the capital of the universe
> I was closest to the beauty of the world.

Pavlović writes with great sympathy of a Serbian king, Dushan, whose lifelong ambition was to conquer Constantinople, but who died in the middle of his climactic campaign. In the poem, the hero attains his wish effortlessly, admitted into the city by angels, as if it were heaven. But when he attempts to govern, his minister tells him:

> Evidently I hadn't noticed
> that I had died two hours before reaching the city
> but he added that I was still a welcome guest
> that on the upper landings rooms were awaiting me
> prepared for the night and for my visit in the hereafter.
>
> Ever since, I've had an important position
> in the death senate of Constantinople
> it's no use looking for my tomb in Serbia
> no use desiring a different glory for me.

The strange phrase "death senate" drives home the ambiguity. The city is the source of death, as it is the source of life-wasting resentment and longing, for Dushan; yet it is also the polis of the mind, the place where the immortals dwell together, regardless of their earthly fortune. Constantinople becomes a parable of the uninhabitable (hence, in its political incarnations, false) ideal. And indeed, all images of a stable ideal, of eternity, seem touched by the same doubleness, in Pavlović. A wonderful poem on "The Last Supper"—spoken, I think, by the fading images of Leonardo's fresco—ends with the same blending of salvation and sterility:

> We have crossed over the water without drinking,
> but everything in paradise is dry.[7]

While I was writing the above paragraphs on Pavlović, I found the same hesitation between the barbarous outlands and "the capital of the universe" expressed, in almost the same language, in a fascinating new poem, "Bypassing Rue Descartes," by the Nobel Prize winner Czeslaw Milosz.[8] Milosz recalls his first arrival in Paris, "A young barbarian just come to the capital of the world." On the one hand, he felt unbounded expectation, a sense of having "entered the universal," in the full philosophical meaning of the term. On the other hand, there was enormous shame at "the customs of our homes," encompassing both religion ("Choral prayers") and naked class distinctions ("The clapping for servants, barefooted girls hurry in"), "About which nobody here should ever be told." In the world as Milosz has experienced it since, both sets of values—the "universal" and the chauvinistic or superstitious—have led to crime, as both have led to suffering and martyrdom:

> Soon enough, many from Jassy and Koloshvar, or Saigon or Marakesh
> Would be killed because they wanted to abolish the customs of their homes.
>
> Soon enough, their peers were seizing power
> In order to kill in the name of the universal, beautiful ideas.

For the older poet, returning, the city retains its sensual fascination, "Rustling with throaty laughter in the dark"; yet he now feels that the very idea of a "capital of the world," a gathering together of all values, carries in it the seed of the exhaustion and dissolution of value. The city remains

> Indifferent as it was to honor and shame and greatness and glory,
> Because that had been done and had transformed itself
> Into monuments representing nobody knows whom,
> Into arias hardly audible or into turns of speech.

In the end, there is a kind of nihilistic balance: "the abolished customs are"—not quite justified, but—"restored to their small fame," because everything is part of a cycle, and "There is no capital of the world, neither here nor anywhere else."

It seems to me a significant fact, in this context, that so much good recent European poetry has come from areas that, like Milosz's Lithuania, Pavlović's Yugoslavia, or Cavafy's Alexandria, are not quite nations, being inhabited by an inextricable mixture of peoples, and handed back and forth, through history, among innumerable conquerors. It is a kind of unsaying of the old D'Annunzian equation between the great Romantic poet and resurgent nationalism. Very near the Lithuania of the, by language and reputation, Polish poet Milosz, is another not-quite-country, East Prussia, whose great recent poet would be classsed as a German—Johannes Bobrowski. In Bobrowski's work, the theme of nationalism, as against the tolerant mix of his homeland, where "Poles, Lithuanians, Russians and Germans lived together and, among them all, the Jews," is handled from a peculiar angle of guilt and complicity.[9] Bobrowski was a common soldier in the Nazi army on the eastern front, and suffered a kind of spiritual paralysis ("Sleep struck us / at the bloody wall") from the acts witnessed, if not performed, there. His poems are a long act of penitential restoration through description. They approach the landscape of his homeland with an old-fashioned lyricism, an old, immensely slowed and trustful sense of space and time, which is itself a constant reminder of how much the war has put into question. In a poem that nowhere mentions the Holocaust, but that everywhere takes resonance from it, "The Jewish Dealer A. S." speaks:

> I am from Rasainen.
> That is where you spend the second night
> in the wood when you come from the river,
> where the woods open
> and yellowish sand
> presses up in the meadows.
>
> There the nights are light.
> Our wives extinguish the fires
> early. We breathe
> long and deep with the dark
> aimless sigh of the wind.

Yet one finally feels that this poetic dwelling-into the land, which is Bobrowski's characteristic note, is at least as much hopeful as it is elegiac or desperate. At the heart of his work is a kind of myth of the marriage—the indissoluble interpenetration—of the landscape and the cultures that have vanished into it, all the way back to prehistory. As in Pavlović, language is the most irrefutable witness and preserver of this union. In the beautiful but slightly sinister poem "Dead Language," which I quote in its entirety, the very weight and sound of words seems itself to contain the abiding animistic presence:

> He with the beating wings
> outside who brushes the door,
> that is your brother, you hear him.
> *Laurio* he says, water,
> a bow, colourless, deep.
>
> He came down with the river,
> drifting around mussel
> and snail, spread like a fan
> on the sand and was green.
>
> *Warne* he says and *wittan*,
> the crow has no tree,
> I have the power to kiss you,
> I dwell in your ear.
>
> Tell him you do not
> want to listen—
> he comes, an otter, he comes
> swarming like hornets, he cries,
> a cricket, he grows with the marsh
> under your house, he whispers
> in the well, *smordis* you hear,
> your black alder will wither
> and die at the fence tomorrow.

The menacing intrusiveness of nature throughout this poem, the black magic at the end, make one realize that the ground Bobrowski seeks to return to, though life-giving, is morally ambivalent. The point is an important one, I think. Given his central subject, there is astonishingly little playing off of the good primitive against the bad late-civilized in Bobrowski's poetry. Indeed, as one bitter poem, "Pruzzian Elegy," acknowledges, the Nazi ethos is itself a product of the primitive ground, or at least its "echo rotting." "Under the linden," a long but all too coherent history has unfolded, from the "groves" that "had smoked with sacrifice" through the many versions of "the strange / god's mother," "her / armoured might," and "the Son's / gallows." It is true that Bobrowski distinguishes sharply between the primitive and the decadent versions: "So when the deep bells / break, a cracked / tinkle remains." But the very fact that he finds the one, in potential, within the other makes his sense of the value of local culture—indeed, of any cultural equilibrium among the ambivalent forces of life—a more searching and unsentimental one; a stance, as "Pruzzian Elegy" puts it, of "angry love."

When I search for an equivalent to this stance in contemporary poetry written in English, I think neither of the sometimes simplistic or amoral affirmations of the primitive in Ted Hughes or Robert Bly; nor of the psychologically profound, but profoundly critical and alienated, visions of Robert Lowell or Sylvia Plath; but of the poetry of Seamus Heaney, and especially of his best book, *North*. That Heaney should be our one point of contact with a spirit prevalent in Eastern European writing is not particularly surprising. He writes out of a country, Northern Ireland, that has been thoroughly Balkanized, its identity torn to pieces in a war that is not simply civil, nor simply religious, nor (propagandists to the contrary) simply colonial, but all three at once. He writes of this war at once as an involved party—Catholic by descent and, at times, by a quite personal sense of humiliation and grievance—and yet, again and again, as a disinterested voice of humanistic conscience.

At the center of *North* is an extended comparison—almost a Joycean mythic parallel—between the war in Northern Ireland and the archaeological discoveries, mostly victims of execution or human sacrifice, found in peat bogs across northern Europe. The theme is first declared in a poem from Heaney's previous volume *Wintering Out*, "The Tollund Man": "Some day I will go to Aarhus / To see his peat-brown head, / The mild pods of his eye-lids." The critic Calvin Bedient has faulted these opening lines for their "polite," touristy flavor; but in fact that very tone prepares a long-drawn-out irony.[10] The poet does not need to go to Aarhus, because Ireland is a living museum of the bog: its dark, seeping, hidden energies, the almost arbitrary victims demanded by its gods. At the end of the poem, after recalling some Northern Irish atrocities, Heaney again imagines his future journey, and says,

> Out there in Jutland
> In the old man-killing parishes
> I will feel lost,
> Unhappy and at home.

What is most difficult and interesting about Heaney's mythic parallel is the tone or attitude with which it is advanced. It is not pure satire; it is certainly not a Lawrencean exculpation, by appeals to the "blood"; but it is something much more tricky. In the poem "Punishment," when Heaney imagines the Stone Age adulteress being led to execution—how the wind "blows her nipples / to amber beads"—one feels, amid the horror and pity, an element of sadistic sexual participation. And when he turns to the modern instance— the tarring and feathering of Catholic girls who have consorted with the enemy—his self-division becomes anguished and overt:

> I who have stood dumb
> when your betraying sisters,
> cauled in tar,
> wept by the railings,
>
> who would connive
> in civilized outrage
> yet understand the exact
> and tribal, intimate revenge.

Even the language here is paradoxical, turned against itself. One "connives," usually, at a crime; but one can connive at being "civilized," if the civility is hypocritical—either because it does not lead to action, or because one secretly sympathizes with the candid, "exact" spirit of primitive pride and retaliation.

The moral thrust of Heaney's invocation of the primitive may be clarified if we look at an instance in which he openly casts himself as mythmaker or legislator—the imaginary ceremony at the center of "Funeral Rites." The passage needs to be quoted entire, if its tone, or tones, are to be assessed accurately:

Now as news comes in
of each neighborly murder
we pine for ceremony,
customary rhythms:

the temperate footsteps
of a cortege, winding past
each blinded home.
I would restore

the great chambers of Boyne,
prepare a sepulchre
under the cupmarked stones.
Out of side-streets and bye-roads

purring family cars
nose into line,
the whole country tunes
to the muffled drumming

of ten thousand engines.
Somnambulent women,
left behind, move
through emptied kitchens

imagining our slow triumph
towards the mounds.
Quiet as a serpent
in its grassy boulevard

the procession drags its tail
out of the Gap of the North
as its head already enters
the megalithic doorway.

Once again, the poet's feelings seem to pull him in different directions. The passage is not satire; yet satire is evident, mildly in the "purring family cars," blackly in "neighborly murder" or "blinded home." It is even there in the final stanza, with the suggestion that Ireland is burying its head, ostrich-like, in the savage past. And when Heaney takes on the role of mythmaker, there is, even in the line break ("I would restore / the great chambers"), that diffidence and self-irony which Bedient dislikes, and I prize as the indication of a skeptical consciousness, an experimenter approaching truth through hypothetical fictions.

And yet, all the same, there is an unavoidable grandeur in the image of the ceremony; as there is enormous compassion in the picture of the "Somnambulent women" who might be consoled by its "slow," "quiet" rhythms. Perhaps the poem, at its most serious level, encompassing both satire and consolation, is saying something like this: we *are* savages; and yet, unlike true savages, we have only our surface justifications, not a "ceremony" that would acknowledge and purge our deepest motives. The last section of the poem suggests that such a ceremony—such a clarified collective consciousness—might mitigate the desire for vengeance, not so much through insight as through a kind of tragic catharsis. "The cud of memory" is "allayed," "arbitration," as well as "the feud" itself, "placated," by the image of

> those under the hill
>
> disposed like Gunnar
> who lay beautiful
> inside his burial mound,
> though dead by violence
>
> and unavenged.

Thus Heaney, like Pavlović, offers an image of the poet who, while he cannot "redeem the time," can mitigate its deadly surface seriousness by his knowledge of timeless motives and the means for assuaging them. To put it differently, acknowledgment of the primitive may be the only beginning of freedom both from the primitive and from the ideological. Like Pavlović, and like Bobrowski, Heaney places a high value on language because, even before it is made into poetry, it is a compressed version of this knowledge. Etymology is archaelogy; witness Heaney's meditation on the old epithet for the body, "bone-house":

> In the coffered
> riches of grammar
> and declensions
> I found *ban-hus*,
>
> its fire, benches,
> wattle and rafters
> where the soul
> fluttered a while
>
> in the roofspace.
> There was a small crock
> for the brain,
> and a cauldron
>
> of generation
> swung at the centre:
> love-den, blood-holt,
> dream-bower.

Language, like the bog, leads us down into our own bodies, into nature, as it leads us back into the past. In this underworld, we find energy and joy, but also reasons for wariness— the sense that it is hard, and necessary, for the fluttering soul to know where (and what) it is, in the house of the self.

In all of the poets we have been discussing, the sense of what poetry can accomplish politically is very limited—at best a bulwark, certainly not a spearhead. But we might do well to remember that these poets (Northern Irish and Eastern European) often have power, in a sense in which American poets very rarely do. People who wish the political reality less grim and rigid than it is read them, and take comfort from them; those who maintain the rigidity pay them the compliment of hatred. It is perhaps too easy to say that these poets' claims are tenacious but minimal *because* they have so much experience of the resistance of reality; or that American political poetry is often sweeping or smug because our words lack consequences. But the contrast is there, and it is worth pondering.

III

In Eugenio Montale's great poem about Florence at twilight, "Times at Bellosguardo"—written during the 1930s, and tinged with the forebodings of that decade—one encounters two extraordinary lines, which could only have been written by a European poet of this century:

> it is too sad
> that so much peace should gather only by glints.

The third and last theme I wish to introduce, in this discussion of values, is the power a poetry of happiness can paradoxically take ("so much peace") from an admission of the limits, and even the ultimate frustration, of happiness. It is not, God knows, that one would want all happy poems to begin "it is too sad"; but that an honesty, and therefore a freedom, accrues from the treatment of happiness within the context of a full consciousness hedged by doubts, other awareness, neurotic and social pressures. The strain, often found in our poetry, of trying to turn even fleeting happiness into dogma or revelation is thereby avoided.

A superb example of all of this can be found in another Montale poem from the 1930s, "Boats on the Marne." The subject is a Sunday excursion on the river, out of sight, but not quite out of hearing, of "the city" with its "sluggish drone."[11] The opening poses the problem of happiness as abandonment, as self-escape—becoming light and weightless as a cork: "The bliss of cork yielding [*abbandonato*] / to the current." There is a feeling of endless motion toward a nature, or a magical realm, which remains endlessly out of reach:

> With oarstrokes you follow the field if the
> butterfly catcher's net will reach it,

and the thicket topping the wall where
dragon's-blood repeats in the cinnabar.

(The enjambments which reinforce the sense of elusiveness
are also there in the Italian.)

Yet out of the day on the river grows the image of a vague,
categorical "the dream"—the encompassing dream of human
beings, the poem almost seems to say. It is a dream at once of
"splendor" and of security, of a "day" that by "recasting" itself
endlessly, like the river, resembles the timeless:

> This is the dream: a vast
> unending day that nearly motionless
> recasts its splendor between the banks,
> and men's good works at every turn,
> a veiled tomorrow that holds no terror.

Perhaps because of the hidden pressure of fear ("what is / the
name of the void that invades us"), sensibility blends almost
seamlessly with historical awareness. "The dream" becomes the
dream of liberal humanism, an agricultural and cultural "good
work," a humanizing of world and psyche, so complete that the
turns of history will hold no surprises, no veiled "terror." Yet
the poem immediately wants to leap beyond the social, as it has
leapt beyond the merely aesthetic. But as soon as the poet tries
to define his—presumably religious—"more," he is left, won-
derfully, back with the precious and fugitive particulars:

> And the dream was something more, but its echo
> fixed on the fleeting waters under
> the penduline's nest, airy and aloof,
> sank like silence in the afternoon's
> concert of cries and evening was a longer
> morning, the great commotion
> great rest.

The ideal is, in a sense, most nearly achieved at the moment
when it is given up.

The ending of the poem is a beautifully suspended one, in
a number of ways. The speaker does not quite hear the banal,

and repeated, words of his companion. (Indeed, it is only at the very end, in a parenthesis, that Montale lets drop the occasion for the day on the river: "your birthday." The instinct for privacy is touching; yet the concealment, along with the unheard speech, cannot help but introduce into the poem a retrospective theme of human isolation—another of the persistent limits of Montalean happiness.)

At the end, the river gathers to its "outlet . . . in a single gush"; yet there is still freedom, still permission, still the blessed corklike aimlessness:

> Evening is like this. Now we can drift downstream
> till the Great Bear kindles.

This last image is itself a suspensive one: we can take it as continuing the pastoral "dream," the attractiveness of letting oneself be guided by natural time rather than clock time; or we can hear undertones of bestial violence and fire—an emblem, like the "enduring color / of the rat" earlier, of what is actually ahead in history.

This ability to make a kind of ecstasy so real while reminding us both of its elusiveness and of its place within a full, hence burdened, human consciousness, is perhaps the most distinctive and unprecedented element in Montale's achievement as a poet. But since I feel it has become, to some degree, typical, in more recent European poetry, I would like to offer one further example, from the poet I began with, Tomas Tranströmer. This example has the additional advantage—being slighter, more purely imagistic, and more naive in tone than Montale's poem—of being closer to much current American practice; it thus offers an occasion for some useful concluding comparisons. (The poem is called "Slow Music," suggesting that a certain intellectual vivacity is deliberately not attempted.) I quote Robert Bly's translation, from *Friends, You Drank Some Darkness:*

> The building not open today. The sun crowds in
>   through the windowpanes
> and warms the upper side of the desk
> which is strong enough to bear the fate of others.

Today we are outdoors, on the long wide slope.
Some have dark clothes. If you stand in the sun, and
  shut your eyes,
you feel as if you were being slowly blown forward.

I come too seldom down to the sea. But now I have come,
among good-sized stones with peaceful backs.
The stones have been gradually walking backwards out
  of the sea.

One thing to notice is that the poem begins by placing the moment of release in the context of our life in society. Though the poet is obviously glad to leave that life behind, he handles it with his characteristically complex irony, not with dismissive satire. In one sense, the third line says the opposite of what it means: it takes far too little conscious strength, or seriousness, for the bureaucrat to make decisions vital to "the fate of others." But in another sense the line is straightforward, and compassionate: our sense of the heaviness of work comes partly from this guilt—or responsibility—whether we accept it or evade it.

The rest of the poem—the turning from society to nature, the moment of release—is harder to carry off successfully, given its million Romantic or sentimental precursors. But it triumphs, I think, through the tact and balance with which Tranströmer defines what such experiences actually give him. It is all there, really, in the feeling of "being slowly blown forward," abandoning oneself even though the goal can neither be attained nor defined. (Though there is a sense of remerging with origins, the sun, the sea.) Even in the middle of this happiness there is ruefulness and self-dissatisfaction ("I come too seldom down to the sea"); but also a self-forgiving determination not to let these feelings intrude too much on the moment ("But now I have come"). The experience is accepted unquestioningly; but it is less a resolution than one pole of life, as the stones' exposure to another element at low tide ("walking backwards out of the sea" as the speaker is "slowly blown forward") is one half of their existence. The poet observes the stones, humanizes them a little, feels comradely with them in his slow contentment; he does not become them.

Set beside a poem like this, most of the obviously compara-
ble American poems seem to me to do at once too much and
too little. Since a poor example would make the case too easily,
let me offer one which, despite what I am about to say, I'm
rather fond of, James Wright's "Today I Was So Happy, So I
Made This Poem":

> As the plump squirrel scampers
> Across the roof of the corncrib,
> The moon suddenly stands up in the darkness,
> And I see that it is impossible to die.
> Each moment of time is a mountain.
> An eagle rejoices in the oak trees of heaven,
> Crying
> *This is what I wanted.*

This poem is like a Gothic spire: it is in such a hurry to get
beyond the earthbound level of feeling or reasoning that it
requires not only surrealism (placing the "oak trees" in "hea-
ven") but flat contradiction of rational experience ("it is impos-
sible to die"). There is something gestural and incomplete—
though very lovably so—about the reach of this poem, its inabil-
ity to let the experience of being "so happy" remain in an
uninterpreted middle ground. Tranströmer's poem, by con-
trast, seems a little saddened and muted, but very assured in its
power to encompass, to provide delicately adequate metaphors
for, what the experience has meant. The strong voice-tone, the
rueful or humorous quality of the third and seventh lines,
helps a great deal. When we know that someone who talks as we
do has had such experiences, we remember more vividly that
we have had them. (I choose Wright as my contrast to Trans-
trömer because he, and the poets usually grouped with him,
seem the closest in style. But I think the problem of dealing
seriously with happiness, short of the terms of religious ecstasy,
is a common American one: we find it in Roethke, in Ginsberg,
even in the Lowell of *Notebook* and *The Dolphin*.)

Can American poets learn anything directly from contem-
porary European poetry? I would say we can at least learn a
way of mixing modes and subjects we have customarily kept
apart; exaltation and the burden of full consciousness; intelli-

gence, cultural reference, and the wild or deep intuitive image; nature—our place in it, our need for it—and the life we mostly live, among man-made things. In writing of history and politics, we can learn a combination of concern and stoical, clear-eyed detachment—the long view—which has been very difficult for us, so that our poetry rarely includes politics without appending itself to a cause, radical or reactionary. We might learn, too, from the archaeological sensibility of poets like Heaney or Pavlović, that a love of language and an interest in the primitive are not necessarily opposites; that language is not, as Adrienne Rich has said and others have implied, the property of an "oppressor" ego.

In a curious sense, the values I am advocating are our old friends from the heyday of the New Criticism: complexity; irony (of the subtle, compassionate sort found in Tranströmer); a Keatsian tolerance for contradictions; and a desire to take account of the full range of awareness in a poem. But that very association has led to a neglect of these virtues, by accidentally linking them with a view of poetry as a formal game; a conservative quietism; an unexploratory playing with paradoxes. Not the least important thing which reading foreign poetry can do for us is to purge away such arbitrary and time-bound associations; and, in the process, to show us a new way of using our intelligence in poetry, without forfeiting other kinds of power.

Notes

This essay, when it was published in 1984, drew a (to me) surprising number of letters of protest. It stung, in a very old way, by suggesting that anything European could be superior to anything American. My intention had been simply to recommend a different kind of approach to political or historical poetry. As I hope the two "Poetry and Politics" essays make clear, I have found a wealth of such poetry in America in the last decade; so I hope the Europe versus America issue, if it had any reality in relation to this piece, can be laid to rest. I have reconsidered a couple of judgments about James Wright; but have decided to let the overall argument speak for the time, and the place in my own development, from which it was written.

1. All quotations are taken from Robin Fulton's translation, in Tomas Tranströmer, *Selected Poems* (Newcastle upon Tyne: Bloodaxe Books, 1987), 121–23.

2. *Truth Barriers* (Sierra Club Books, 1980), 9.

3. The quotations come from Robert Bly's translation in *Friends, You Drank Some Darkness* (Boston: Beacon Press, 1975), 199.

4. "About History," Fulton, 75–76.

5. *Another Republic,* ed. Charles Simic and Mark Strand (Boston: Beacon Press, 1976), 17.

6. There is a superb French translation by Robert Marteau, *La Voix sous la pierre* (Paris: Gallimard, 1970). The quotations here come from Joachim Neugroschel's renderings—largely based on Marteau—in the chapbook *The Conqueror in Constantinople* (N.P.: New Rivers Press, 1976). Further englishings of Marteau, by me and Richard Tillinghast, appeared in *Ploughshares* 7, no. 2 (1981).

7. I quote from my own translation, *Ploughshares* 7, no. 2 (1981): 64–65.

8. "Bypassing Rue Descartes," trans. Renata Gorczynski and Robert Hass, *New Republic,* 23 May 1981, 30.

9. Quoted in Michael Hamburger's foreword to *Shadow Land: Selected Poems of Johannes Bobrowski,* trans. Ruth and Matthew Mead (London: Donald Carroll, 1966). All my quotations come from this text. An American edition was published by Ohio University Press, but is now unavailable.

10. Calvin Bedient, "The Music of What Happens," *Parnassus* (fall–winter 1979), 111.

11. My quotations come from the translation by Sonia Raiziss and Alfredo de Palchi in Eugenio Montale, *Selected Poems* (New York: New Directions, 1965).

III

III

My Father's T. S. Eliot and Mine

My father won his copy of *The Waste Land* in a poker game in Pullman, Washington, in the 1920s. Years later, his students at the University of Chicago believed that his tan leather attaché case—a "wonderful ratty old thing"—was a gift from T. S. Eliot. This was not true, of course; but it shows how profoundly his shyness and reserve, his dark tweeds, the conservative emotions underneath his Stevensonian political liberalism, had aligned him with the poet he idolized all his life. "It was like studying Eliot with Eliot," Robert Langbaum once told me. If my father was, in some sense, Eliot's vicar, he saw Eliot largely as Eliot wanted to see himself: a poet who fulfilled the dictates of his own criticism; who had restored a culture of the whole mind, including wit, satire, and "a direct sensuous apprehension of thought," after decades of easy Victorian loftiness. Though my father knew that Eliot's poetry was not altogether "impersonal," he did not pursue the subject very far, at least not in public.

My father's friendship with Eliot was real. In 1931, he and my mother had actually been to 9 Clarence Gate Gardens, and had seen Vivien put her face down on the table, shielded by her hands, for several minutes during dinner, while Mr. Eliot (he was never called "Tom," in my hearing) talked on all the more brilliantly, as if to persuade them that nothing was happening. In later years, the friendship was hampered by my father's reluctance to put himself forward, his disdain for anything that smacked of using people or

---

Presented at the annual meeting of the Modern Language Association in 1988.

"playing the game." When Eliot visited Chicago for the last time, in 1959, under the auspices of *Poetry* magazine, Henry Rago, then its editor, did not invite my father to the huge reception, crammed with socialites. Deeply stung, my father made no attempt to contact Eliot during that visit. And I guess that is why it was not with him, but with my honors English class, that I sat and heard Eliot, far below in the gold light of Orchestra Hall.

Intentionally or not, that reading now seems like a reliving of the "pattern of timeless moments" in Eliot's life as a poet: first "Prufrock," which *Poetry* had printed, though only at Ezra Pound's insistence. Then "The Hippopotamus"—though Eliot said he was reading it by request, and no longer understood it. Then came the inspired section of *The Waste Land,* written in the clinic at Lausanne; then the Earthly Paradise of "Marina" and *Ash Wednesday* part VI, through which Lyndall Gordon has so movingly followed the spoor of the not-at-all-impersonal T. S. Eliot. And finally, the great intoning voice ending on the ending of "East Coker," which so weirdly mocked "the wisdom of old men," and seemed to side with my own adolescent eagerness and terror:

> Old men ought to be explorers
> Here and there does not matter
> We must be still and still moving
> Into another intensity
> For a further union, a deeper communion
> Through the dark cold and the empty desolation,
> The wave cry, the wind cry, the vast waters
> Of the petrel and the porpoise.   In my end is my
>   beginning.

I am sure I could not have had the same experience of that reading if my father had been there. And the Eliot who emerged for me—indeed, became my idea of poetry itself— that autumn is not primarily the one I find in my father's criticism. For me, Eliot represented a kind of slipping-space between accepted levels of reality. The beginning of *The Waste Land,* where real voices emerged from, and sank back into, the deep voice facing inward, toward the dream-truths of the central self. *Ash Wednesday,* where the language of self-examination turned into the incantatory language of ritual, and then the strange visions emerged—the three white leopards under the juniper tree, the figure climbing in the abandoned tower—as under the beat of a shaman's drum. The *Quartets,* where a kind of sign was set on a real place making it a place which was "the world's end," and the generating point of a universe of wildly various poetries. Eliot stood for, and fed, a kind of dissatisfaction with discourse except in so far as it flowed into and out of other functions of the mind. The fragmentation of story and saying—far from representing the "chaos" of the "modern world"—relieved story and saying of the, for me, boring triviality of their place in the seamless managing of the adult world, and made them coextensive with intuited Truth. It was an experience that would come back in the discourse of lovers, of close friends, of psychoanalysis; but it came to me, at fifteen, in Eliot's poetry. One of my imaginary projects that fall was a movie of the first twenty lines of *The Waste Land,* that would enact, still more vividly, their truth to the metamorphoses of consciousness.

The other side of Eliot that appealed to me greatly was his assertion that poetry was "beyond beauty and ugliness," and his application of that to the urban landscape. The Chicago through which I found my way home after his reading, on the clanking IC train (it was the first time in my life that I had been downtown at night without my parents), would not have struck most people as a beautiful, or a safe, place. But it was a haunted place for me, especially as it unconsciously symbolized the loneliness of setting out on my own in the world. It was this element that dominated in the poems I wrote that fall, of which I can still quote four or five lines:

> Secular Advent,
> December deepening in the frozen earth,
> December of decayed leaves, December of pale sunsets,
> December of smashed stone and bent iron along railroad
>   tracks,
> Now in the unsheathed sun bending toward solstice.

But it was more than the city, and loneliness; Eliot had taught the importance of the negative, of haunted feelings as well as beautiful ones, in the economy of soul making as well as in truthfulness about the world. (So, of course, had Wordsworth, but I did not take that into account as yet.) And so, when I read Louis Untermeyer's description of Eliot's "inverted romanticism masked as classicism," it struck me not as the snide put-down it now seems, but as a profound truth I knew my father would hate. "Romanticism" meant inwardness, that afterglow of the unconscious Eliot gave to everything; "inverted" meant including the negative, the "destructive element."

Was my perception of Eliot merely an accident of who I was, who my father was, and the partly vocal, partly tacit struggle between us? Or was it a sea change Eliot himself had gone through, making him available in a different way to a different generation? Let me offer in evidence a poem by one of the poets I had hoped would be here today—and who declined with regret, affirming Eliot's importance for her— Jorie Graham's "Pollock and Canvas." It is a poem about the desire for an art beyond art, an art all slippage and impossibly full Truth, and how dangerously that desire pushes the artist toward not touching the canvas at all. In the midst of this meditation on Pollock, a story suddenly intrudes, that will seem hauntingly familiar to most readers:

> The king can neither ride nor walk, neither lie nor stand, he
>   leans but cannot sit and sighs
> remembering. . . .
>   There is a lake, they bring him there for the
>   air for his painful open wound, he calls it his
> hunting day.

This is, of course, the figure of Amfortas from Wagner's *Parsifal*, who had suffered an unhealing sexual wound when he allowed the sacred Lance to be stolen; the same figure who, in Eliot, goes to a river and is called the "fisher king." Amfortas's entrance is followed, in Graham's poem, by a section written in numbered one-line stanzas. These are the first fifteen:

1
Here is the lake, the open, he calls it his day; fishing.
2
The lake, the middle movement, woman's flesh, maya.
3
And here is the hook before it has landed, before it's deep in
   the current,
4
the hovering—keeping the hands off—the gap alive,
5
the body of talk between the start and beauty,
6
all limbs this one sucked alive by delay and brought to stand
   here in the room among the rest of the forms
7
this girl all accident all *instead-of*, of the graces the
8
most violent one, the one all gash, all description,
9
(between the creator and the created: a flash: a girl)
10
(the most violent one) (*one cannot produce depth only the sensation
   of depth*)
11
(without embarrassment, without shame) the most violent
   one—
12
as in *I can* (the hook hissing mid-air) *control the flow of paint,
   there is no accident no beginning no end. . . .*
13
Oh but we wanted to paint what is not beauty, how can one
   paint what is not beauty . . . ?
14
And I will cover thee with my hand when I pass by
15
And will take away my hand and thou shalt see my back my
16
form—

What is of Eliot in this, other than the fisher king himself? It
is, I would argue, the montage-like slipping between levels, so
different—as Guy Davenport has shown—from the crisp junc-

tures of the Poundian ideogram. The wounded king casting his line toward the water *is* the psychically wounded Jackson Pollock casting his brush toward the canvas. "The lake" is "the open," the uncompromised potential, so valued by the action painters; it is also the Muse, the female figure of embodiment who is both temptress and goal, like Kundry in the opera. But these appositions are accomplished by syntactic glide, not statement—as, in "Burnt Norton," the rose garden turns from a metaphor to a real place by glides. Allusion, too, is plentiful, but always brought in obliquely, creating troubling, suggestive half-equivalences. Line 10 reads:

> (the most violent one) (*one cannot produce depth only the
> sensation of depth*)

One could say, paraphrasing, that the quotation from Pollock, attacking representation, proves that his muse is "the most violent one"; but that would miss the dreamlike quickness of the connection. So Marie Larisch's voice emerges out of "April is the cruellest month"; so "the heart of light, the silence" equals, or else opposes, "*Oed' und leer das Meer.*"

It might sound too glib to say that Graham is also in Eliot's tradition because she is an experimenter, and her experiments annoy people: those numbered one-line stanzas, those blanks left, apparently, because no adequate word exists. But her experiments, like Eliot's, are pressures against the very idea of the aesthetic—but not know-nothing defiant randomness, rather pressures that increase nerve and intensity. "Oh but we wanted to paint what is not beauty" is a cry she shares with Eliot, and, in both cases, it turns toward religion: the story of Moses, who is allowed to hide and glimpse Jahweh's back, because Jahweh's face would annihilate him.

I think I could adduce similar examples, from Allen Grossman, Frank Bidart, Louise Glück; perhaps even from my own ideas about how to go about constructing a long poem. If I am correct, and my adolescent perceptions are in some way generalizable, then Eliot's influence may be the great undiscussed secret of contemporary poetry, for all the talk of Pound, Williams, Stevens, and Moore. The reasons for such a silence would not be far to seek. Eliot is in bad odor because of his supposed influence on the poets of the 1940s, whose work has almost no montage, no slippage between conscious and unconscious, but a great deal of social wit, and a fusion of feeling and thought that has come more to mean the interrogation of feeling by thought. Of course, as David Perkins has pointed out, it was Eliot's criticism, not his poetry, that shaped the work of Wilbur, Nemerov, and their contemporaries. But an insistence like my father's that Eliot's criticism and his practice were one might seem to have contributed to the process. So I would like to go back and look at what my father actually said, and the circumstances under which he said it. For I do not wish to leave the impression that my generation has somehow rescued a true Eliot from the misconceptions of earlier generations.

This fall, I read through my father's 1929 monograph, *The Talent of T. S. Eliot,* which, short though it is, was the first book ever published on Eliot. Not long before, I had visited the campus of the University of Oregon, where my father was teaching when he wrote it, after his stint at Pullman. The campus reminded me a little of my own Eastern college, Haverford—a hodgepodge of architectural styles made beautiful by the density of tall, shaggy trees. But my mother said the trees were saplings when my father taught there; and the hodgepodge was perhaps too much a hodgepodge, an exact replica of a French Hotel de Ville housing the science amphitheaters. It seemed a part of the country poised between rawness and sophistication, where *The Waste Land* could easily change hands in a poker game. What would such a place have meant to a young Midwestern Swede who had grown up all over the West, and come to the intellectual world by his own efforts? I imagine there was a sense of culture as something that had to be built, and could be built wrong. This must have felt answered by the sense that great moments in poetry are also built—out of the responses one has had to the same situation in the great works of the past, out of the rigorous examination of an important philosopher, until at last the definitive statement of a predicament stands free. "For example, this passage," my father wrote:

> I have heard the key
> Turn in the door once and turn once only
> We think of the key, each in his prison
> Thinking of the key, each confirms a prison
> Only at nightfall, aetherial rumours
> Revive for a moment a broken Coriolanus

Here we have allusions to Dante and Shakespeare—allusions that have the quality of experiences—and a substructure of idealism drawn from Bradley's *Appearance and Reality*. And yet this is the same "direct sensuous apprehension of thought" that Eliot notes in Donne. How implicit the thought is in the feeling may be seen by comparing this passage with Arnold's "Self-Dependence," where the thought is similar but smaller.

I looked up the Arnold poem, and one quite takes my father's point:

> From the intense, clear, star-sown vault of heaven,
> Over the lit sea's unquiet way,
> In the rustling night-air came the answer:
> "Wouldst though *be* as these are? *Live* as they.
>
> "Unaffrighted by the silence round them,
> Undistracted by the sights they see,
> These demand not that the things without them
> Yield them love, amusement, sympathy.

The thought here could hardly be less "implicit" in the feeling. What a hectoring, Rugby-Chapel tone it is delivered in! And how stagily it is hung onto the stars! A little like that Hotel de Ville plunked down on the science classrooms. (Of course, the 1920s are never quite fair to the Victorians. If my father had chosen "To Marguerite"—really much closer to *The Waste Land* in its anguish over solipsism—the case would have been much harder.)

My father goes on to treat Eliot's metrics, too, as a matter of subtle construction—he uses Grierson's phrase "bold, irregular fingering"—rather than either "free verse" or Miltonic sonority. And here there is a striking, speculative sentence, built like many around a quotation from Eliot, which I think embodies the overriding myth of my father's essay: "The study of Donne provoked Eliot to assert that 'a style, a rhythm, to be significant, must embody a significant mind'—a thought which must have come to Donne as he looked at the easy Spenserianism of his day." Eliot is to Arnold as Donne is to Spenser, or at least his imitators—recoverers in a perennial war between writing that is alive in all its dimensions and mere "style." Whether the judgments are fair or not, it's hard to overestimate how urgent that sense of recovery was for the critics and poets of the 1920s. The examples my father chooses from Eliot are sufficient proof that he was not looking for the surface argumentative rationality that Yvor Winters, or the poets of the 1940s, valued. But I can imagine my father arguing that it is only because the subtler modes of construction—Eliot's or Donne's or Dante's—have passed into our blood that we can afford to ignore them, and look for other values in poetry.

What I find hardest to enter into sympathetically in my father's essay is the tone of brisk, boyish iconoclasm surrounding Eliot's standard of "tough reasonableness beneath the slight lyric grace." The problem is that one age's toughness may be the next age's narrowness of perspective. Is what resists the "slight lyric grace" of "La Figlia Che Piange" really "tough reasonableness," or a fear of intimacy left largely unexamined? As, in the last few years, we have begun to sift unwarranted rumor from fact, and to see how much personal conflict actually lies behind the most charged images in Eliot's poetry, I wonder if many sympathetic readers my age were deeply surprised. We knew that Eliot's poetry was about soul making; and we knew that the soul is most made in the dark, intolerable passages that will not be found by the "lean solicitor." And for us, it made him a larger, not a smaller, poet—more in the company of Dante and Shakespeare, those poets (to steal from Keats again) whose life was allegory, and whose works were the commentary on it. But I think we should acknowledge (or I, at least, should acknowledge) that there is an element of triumph in appropriating Eliot to our own psychological view of the soul's progress—be it lax or compassionate—and away from the moralistic view that still hung so heavily over his generation, and my father's. Up to a point, this appropriation is justified. Eliot's poetry, as it returns obsessively to the same images, does depict a series of evolving psychological states or psychological capacities; and one quality of the evolution is greater compassion, toward himself and others. I suspect that most of what is wisdom, and not self-complacency, in the advice given in our self-help books could be found somewhere in *The Cocktail Party* or *Four Quartets*. Still, it is only up to a point. One reads "Burnt Norton" one way knowing how "much in love" Eliot was when he visited the rose garden with Emily Hale; one reads it another way when one knows how soon, and how bafflingly, he was withdrawing from her. The Eliot who wished for fewer "free-thinking Jews" in the world, the Eliot who had his beloved's letters burned because she had dared to make his available to a distant posterity, was a very strange man, and very fluent in what I have elsewhere called the "brontosaurian language" of an old severity, duty, and prejudice. Eliot will gather new significances for each succeeding generation, but, like my father, he is not wholly recoverable for any time other than his own. But he had the greatness to say so himself:

And he: "I am not eager to rehearse
  My thought and theory which you have forgotten.
  These things have served their purpose: let them be.
So with your own, and pray they be forgiven
  By others, as I pray you to forgive
  Both bad and good. Last season's fruit is eaten
And the fullfed beast shall kick the empty pail.
  For last year's words belong to last year's language
  And next year's words await another voice."

On the Survival of Pentameter

My taste for formal poetry has always been a rather dark, private, unreasoned, and evasive sort of thing. It has not always dominated my own writing; it certainly hasn't made me feel in any way at war with the great free verse poets of our time. It has made me feel a little defensive: why should it so conclusively exclude me from the avant-garde, when it didn't exclude (say) Hart Crane in 1923? But mainly, I've felt appalled by, and quite disconnected from, the terms in which the argument is conducted, by meter's detractors and, at times, by its defenders. Formal poets, it is presumed, relish the idea of art as a game or a contest. They see the medium as a glorious artifice, whose transparency is, at best, a carefully cultivated illusion. They are also committed to the worst excesses of reason and order. The formal poet, as Galway Kinnell would have it, carries around with him, willy-nilly, the Elizabethan notion that as he designs his poem, so God designed the universe—the "music of the spheres." Such a poet clearly has no place in a post-Einsteinean cosmos where space unpredictably becomes time, and energy matter.

My quarrel with all this is that it is simply not what I hear when I listen to the twentieth-century masters who make me love the formal tradition and wish to be part of it. For me, the great metrical poets of the century are Yeats, Frost, Crane, Stevens, and Lowell: men of large, unruly emotions, who in the area of belief tended to skepticism or else to Dionysiac enthusiasm—certainly not to rational theology. When I listen to:

Ironwood, December 1984.

> O Thou steeled Cognizance whose leap commits
> The agile precincts of the lark's return

or

> When the whale's viscera go and the roll
> Of its corruption overruns this world

or

> And the first flowers upon it, an alphabet
> By which to spell out holy doom and end,
> A bee for the remembering of happiness

or even

> These pools that, though in forests, still reflect
> The total sky almost without defect

what I hear is a shape of yearning, cherishing, or anger *beyond* the rational, whose tremulousness is in some obscure way protected by the fact that it can be fitted into these world-old insistences. The same is true of some of the minor successes of the "confessional" poets, who are often considered old-fashioned, in spite of their subject matter, simply because they stuck with meter as long as they did. My heart still warms to Anne Sexton's lines,

> I needed you. I didn't want a boy,
> only a girl, a small milky mouse
> of a girl, already loved, already loud in the house
> of herself. We named you Joy.
> I, who was never quite sure
> about being a girl, needed another
> life, another image to remind me.
> And this was my worst guilt; you could not cure
> nor soothe it. I made you to find me.

because the meter, and the deliberate, gawky variations on it, tell me how much she means—and how nervous it makes her to say—this potentially banal psychoanalytic discovery about herself. (As Pope observed, much of what good poetry says is banal, because it is true; what matters, the *force* of truth, resides in the saying.)

One thing that meter does, then, is to transmit an urgency of excitement in the voice, by the very pressure with which it brings words together. Another thing it does is somehow to protect the vulnerability of that urgency, by its hypnotic effect, and by the age-old presumption of importance that attaches to it. It gives the poet an initial permission to be as intimate as Sexton, as outlandish in vocabulary and syntax as Hopkins or Crane. It draws a kind of magic circle within which, as in primitive cultures, it is safe to dance out one's possession by the demon, or (as Rilke would say) by the angel.

What, then, is the difference in effect between formal poetry and free verse? Robert Hass, in his essay "Listening and Making," says perhaps the first intelligent thing I have heard said on this subject in twenty years of controversy. He distinguishes two stages in our emotional response to rhythm. The first stage he calls "threshold alertness" or "animal alertness": the state of heightened attention we feel when we suspect a pattern emerging but do not yet recognize it—like an animal lifting its head at an unfamiliar noise in the forest. Then,

> there is often a moment or more of compelled attention in which the play and repetition of the sounds seem—I am pulled toward metaphor again—to draw us in or overwhelm us. That kind of listening can lead to something like trance. It is the feeling out of which comes another set of metaphors—magic, incantation—and practices.

The brilliant application of this is:

> most metrical poems, by establishing an order so quickly, move almost immediately from the stage of listening for an order to the stage of hearing it in dialogue with itself. They suppress animal alertness in the rush to psychic magic and they do so by laying claim to art and the traditions of art at the beginning. The free verse poem insists on the first stage of sensual attention, of possibility and emergence—which is one of the reasons why it has seemed fresher and more individual to the twentieth century.

I have to say I don't like the rhetorical undercurrent of this passage, which is (as becomes explicit a few sentences later) to reintroduce the equation meter = order = traditional thought, thereby proving in advance that free verse is the "fresher" mode for our time. But Hass's truly remarkable insight is simpler, and evaluatively neutral: free verse is "animal alertness"; meter is "psychic magic," "incantation," "trance." The consequences of this perception are, it seems to me, enormous. One conclusion that could be drawn from it is that the battle over form in our time really has little to do with questions of order and liberty. It lies, rather, between those who believe in the curative value of Dionysiac emotional possession and catharsis, and those who believe that emotions interfere with a Zen-like attentiveness, an outward-turning clarity, incomparably to be desired. The great modern free verse innovators do not seem to me "fresher" than their more formal contemporaries; but they do seem cooler, calmer spirits, all "animal alertness." The Zen teacher Shunryu Suzuki wrote, "Because we enjoy all aspects of life as an unfolding of big mind, we do not care for any excessive joy." *That* is the spirit I hear when I listen to

> Cut branches back for a day—
> trail a thin line through willow
> up buckbrush meadows

or

> To be in love is like going out-
> side to see what kind of day
>
> it is

or

> Man looking into the sea,
> taking the view from those who have as much right to it
>   as you have to it yourself,
> it is human nature to stand in the middle of a thing,
> but you cannot stand in the middle of this

or

Flowers through the window
lavender and yellow

changed by white curtains.

A quiet, contemplative attunement to what simply is, edged with irritation at those who persist in intruding themselves, their heartbeats, their iambs, where only "animal alertness" is appropriate.

What I have just argued is, of course, an extreme position, inspired by exasperation with a half-truth that almost everyone writing about poetry seems to believe. A certain amount of modern poetry, both metrical and nonmetrical, flatly contradicts me. A larger body of poetry does not fit because it falls somewhere between the two extremes. Long-line free verse, for example, tends to have more emphatic stresses than short-line, and it often brings in an incantatory element through the repetition of phrases or syntactic structures. So it is not surprising that it has appealed to poets who are passionate as well as spontaneous: Whitman, Jeffers, Ginsberg.

But, as Hass observes, every good poem, on some level, involves a dialogue between elements of regularity and variation, "trance" and "alertness." What I would like to consider now is how pentameter remains a part of this dialogue in modern poetry, even, sometimes, in the places where you would least expect it. The presence of ghost pentameter is regularly noticed in poets who begin by writing in meter and later shift to free verse—Lowell and Plath, for instance. But Hugh Kenner has observed, in *The Pound Era,* that in the very canto in which Pound says, "To break the pentameter, that was the first heave," he moves (Kenner maintains, by way of a history of the line from the Italian hendecasyllabic on) to this famous line:

What thóu lóvest wéll rĕmáins,
the rést is dróss

With Kenner's exegesis in mind, I recently found myself reading another famous modernist passage with different eyes:

Without invention nothing is well-spaced

The junior Philip Levines of the magazines, who arrange
their poems in typewritten columns an inch and a half wide,
all know that this means what Pound meant: pentameter is
finished. That it might mean that *all* good poets need to in-
vent a formal equivalent for an individual sense of how the
world is "spaced"—and thereby cast a disturbing light on
their own practice—does not trouble them. Or the fact that it
is an all-but-perfect pentameter line.

Withŏut invéntiŏn nóthĭng ĭs wéll-spáced

Noticing here what Kenner had noticed about Pound led me
to look through the rest of the passage and to find Williams
dismantling and rebuilding the pentameter line in a seem-
ingly endless struggle. The line comes nearest to disappearing
when Williams is inventing the "threshold alertness" that will
allow the things of the world to hold their salient place in the
reader's imagination:

> the hummocks margining the all
> but spent channel of the old swale,
> the small foot-prints
> of the mice under the overhanging
> tufts of the bunch-grass.

Yet even here, one notices how the lines seem, syntactically, to
press beyond their generally four-stress limits to swallow the
extra word or phrase that would make them pentameter ("the
hummocks margining the all but spent," "the mice under the
overhanging tufts"). At the end, when Williams invokes the
sense of completeness that makes the word "live" because of
its place in the line, he allows himself, for one line, as at the
beginning, the very nostalgia he is abjuring:

> withóut invéntiŏn thĕ líne
> wĭll névĕr ăgáin tăke ón ĭts áncient

divisions when the word, a supple word,
lived in it, crumbled now to chalk.

Then, of course, he takes it back. The last line is charming both because it enacts the crumbling of pentameter, and because it shows the sudden new vividness and sharp edge pentameter can acquire through Poundian spondee, Hopkinsian springing out of unstressed syllables. For, however ironically, this passage is as powerful as it is largely because its invoked, though forbidden, ideal of a satisfying line is the line we all learned in our first encounters with poetry, the line of Shakespeare, Milton, and Keats. I suspect Williams invokes the ghost of that line oftener, in subtler ways, than most of his disciples realize. For instance, the last lines of verse on the immediately preceding page of *Paterson* (before a prose interpolation) read:

Love

                                                  combating sleep

_____

                                                      the sleep

piecemeal

One way of construing this is:

                    Love combating sleep // the sleep piecemeal

The problem with much contemporary poetry is that it has nothing to play off against in this way. The battle for free verse has been so thoroughly won that many younger poets think very little about (and accept mechanical solutions to) the problems of rhythm, lineation, and even sound. As Hass observes in the essay I have been quoting, they prefer to argue about the content of poetry, whether it should be "surrealistic" or sophisticated and self-aware, ignoring the fact that, as Williams says, the irrational and sensuous side of poetry lies largely in the way words "live" within the line.

In such a situation, it is not surprising that some poets have sought richness and liveliness in a return to fairly strict meter. It is not surprising, either, that certain critics have assailed them for bringing back the 1950s; nevertheless, some of the work associated with this revival has real force and distinction. Here is Amy Clampitt, listening to Beethoven and thinking of her Midwestern father:

> the Arietta
> a disintegrating surf of blossom
> opening along the keyboard, along the fencerows
> the astonishment of sweetness. My father,
> driving somewhere in Kansas or Colorado.
> in dustbowl country, stopped the car
> to dig up by the roots a flower
> he'd never seen before—a kind
> of prickly poppy most likely, its luminousness
> wounding the blank plains like desire.

Here is Alfred Corn, describing Santa Fe:

> On brown arms, silver and lumps of turquoise, smoothed
>
> Pace of conduct, deliberate, fated, at one
> With the cloudless sky transfixed by a single
> Crossbeamed silver sun. Completeness, like the rounded
>
> Snow of adobe. Reticence, like the shadows
> In half-seen courtyards.

An old-fashioned feeling of wonder, of caught breath, mingled with a lot of sheer prose intelligence, is the tone here—more passionate than Wilbur, more checked and self-conscious than Crane. The iambic pentameter isn't that exact, either, if one looks at it closely. There is a lot of what Hopkins called counterpoint (falling rhythm, where rising rhythm is expected), and Clampitt even modulates between four- and five-stress lines. This work is much more radical and syncopated than we think of 1950s verse being. If it still falls below the high points of formal verse in this century, the reason is perhaps a slight patina of the beautiful imposed too consistently. Corn's passage, particularly, makes me impatient to hear something about the Indians' poverty or the U.S. government's plans for the uranium on their land; and for poetic, not political, reasons. But the passage has its own kind of exactness and resonance, all the same.

Another possibility, for recent poets, seems to be the use of ghost pentameter in exploring precisely that larger terrain of the factual and the anti-poetic. Here meter functions more as it does in Frost, as a kind of ground bass dramatizing the inherent music of speech, bringing out the intensity in a discourse that might not seem intense otherwise. James McMichael's *Four Good Things* is a good example (and an astonishing book, in the range of anti-poetic subjects—economic history, domestic architecture—it includes). Here is a poignant, quieter passage about the uprootedness of retired Midwesterners in California:

> Their sense of
> where they lived depended strangely on their
> fitness to change, as if they couldn't know
> without those changes where they were or what they
> wanted in their lives. Living here was too much what
> they'd
> thought it would be. The sequences of perfect days were
> unavoidably what they'd come for.

Like Clampitt and Corn, McMichael uses a lot of counterpoint; he also uses many additional weak syllables—even extra feet—and a stress as light, often, as that of Creeley or Williams. For some readers, his lines are simply prose; for others, the prolongations, the peculiar music of suspended line endings (emphasized, here, by long-*a* assonance), the incremental repetitions like "what they / wanted," "what they'd / thought," convey very powerfully how much Crane-like longing has been frustrated in these lives, this speech. I think of Frost's vibrant, timid first line in "A Servant to Servants": "I didn't make you know how glad I was."

Another poet who is radically concerned with the dramatization of speech is Frank Bidart. He seems farther from pentameter than McMichael, because of his penchant for short or

broken lines. But listen to this passage from "The War of
Vaslav Nijinsky":

> Suffering has made me what I am,—
>
> I must not regret; or judge; or
> struggle to escape it
>
> in the indifference of (the ruthless
> ecstacy of)
>   CHANGE; "my endless RENEWAL"; BECOMING.
>
> —That is Nietzsche.
>
> He wants to say "*Yes*" to life.
>
> I am not Nietzsche. I am the bride of Christ.

The first line here is pentameter, as is (allowing for some
fairly normal substitutions) the last—that strange burst of irra-
tional, complexly suggestive conviction:

Í am nŏt nót Niétzschĕ. Í am thĕ bríde ŏf Chríst.

But beyond this, as I listen to the poem, it seems to me that
three of the couplet groupings (ll. 2–3, 4–5, and 7–8) also
add up to loose pentameters. They are trying to build them-
selves toward pentameter, as Nijinsky is trying to think his
way through to a thought that will satisfy him. (When Ni-
jinsky's great inspiration and rival, Nietzsche, reaches the
thought that satisfies *him,* in line 6—"CHÁNGE; mў énd-
lĕss RÉNÉWĂL; BĔCÓMĬNG"—there is a contrasting, mainly
dactylic, falling rhythm, which tells us how doubtful these
phrases sound in Nijinsky's mouth.)

When I point out such effects to undergraduate writing
classes, I am invariably asked whether poets consciously in-
tend them. The answer, of course, is no; but a no hedged with
endless qualifications about the instincts of a good poet, espe-
cially one educated in what we used to call "the tradition." For
such a poet, I would argue, the pentameter line means some-
thing in terms of rest, conviction, resonance of feeling, so that
the poet tends unconsciously to circle back to it when such a

deep satisfaction is sought or found. But this has nothing to do with nostalgia for any particular metaphysical structure; the human experience it refers to is too general and multiform, and can occur in too many contexts of culture or belief. The spirit can rest in "Downward to darkness, on extended wings" as well as in "I am the bride of Christ." Thus Hass is drawn to the primitive metaphor of "trance," I to the primitive metaphor of a magic circle.

To me, these various uses of the traditional line are what is most interesting, from a purely formal point of view, in my own generation's work. But they are interesting, I hasten to qualify, in so far as they are not traditional. As Eliot said, there is no point in exactly repeating a previous generation's artistic solutions. The generation of Wilbur gave meter a bad name largely because it did not do much with meter that had not already been done by Auden, Stevens, or Ransom. Whether poets of my generation have really done something with pentameter that goes beyond the great modernists, or the "confessional" poets, remains to be seen. One straw in the wind might be the prevalence of counterpoint; another, surely, is the tendency in Bidart and McMichael to end lines on words like "of," "their," and "or." For any previous generation, such enjambments would have been a sign of weakness or lack of skill; for this one, they seem the sign of impetus and intensity, of an exacting quest.

So we come back, again, to the dialogue between assertions and disintegrations of form. Another essay could be written on that dialogue with a parti pris for free verse; to a great extent, Hass's "Listening and Making" is that essay. For genuine (as opposed to magazine) free verse can do many things better than metrical poetry can. What it cannot do quite as well—if these are things one wants poetry to do—is convey urgency, nerves, or hypnotic depth of feeling; justify strangeness; and bring the poem to a certain level of peace with itself—as another splendid contemporary formal poet, Allen Grossman, puts it, "Establish rest. Establish rest profound."

The New Audience

A few years ago, I used to visit a Sunday poetry group in a small but prosperous Northern California town. Some of the members—not a majority—were teachers at the local community college. More than half were women, and they tended to have secretarial or low-level managerial jobs, with which they did not feel particularly identified. One of the men (who has since died, I'm sorry to say) was a retired lawyer, who knew Greek and Latin. He was the acknowledged authority on metrics, and saw to it that the visiting speaker got paid. They were a kind, unpretentious group. We would talk about Rilke, Tranströmer, or Larkin (poets most of them had read), and then, a little timidly, they would bring out their own poems. And always, there was the sad, perplexed moment when they would wonder, *Why is there no audience for poetry?*

I heard the same conversations last summer, teaching for the first time at Warren Wilson, an experimental M.F.A. program where people from many professions—who cannot af-

---

This piece, presented at the annual meeting of the Modern Language Association in 1988, was written before Donald Hall's introduction to *The Best American Poetry 1989*, which makes some of the same points, and, of course, before Dana Gioia's "Can Poetry Matter?" If my hypothesis about the 1960s has any merit, Gioia's complaint that poetry has lost the upper- and upper-middle-class audience that patronizes opera, ballet, etc., might rather suggest a *shift* in audiences, as much for political as for aesthetic reasons.

In 1993, the Pulitzer Prize for poetry went to Louise Glück's *The Wild Iris*—ending a remarkable record of neglect of the best poets of a generation.

ford to take more time off from their lives—pay a substantial tuition to come to two ten-day residencies a year, and then work with an established poet or fiction writer by correspondence. My own five students included a lawyer, two school psychologists or counselors, a free-lance editor, and a doctor's wife. And I began to ask myself, why don't these people see that they are the audience they are looking for? That all over the country, in every medium-sized city, there are poetry groups like theirs, often Poetry Centers and reading series, people who go off to writers' conferences and programs like Warren Wilson—and that this would have been all but unthinkable even thirty years ago?

They do not draw this conclusion, I believe, for two reasons. The first is that, from their point of view, *they* are the poets (more about this later). The second is that they are well-educated upper-middle-class people, and tend, in their liberal decency, to assume that a *real* audience would be working-class and poorly educated, rare though such audiences have been in the history of poetry.

How did this new audience come into being? Does its existence affect the best poetry being written now? Is it different in kind from other audiences because, I would guess, about 80 percent of its members aspire in some way to be poets themselves? These are the questions I would like to take up, in the short time available.

As to origins, I believe this is one of many areas in which the cultural effects of the 1960s have been more enduring than the political ones. In the 1950s, poetry readings were given by T. S. Eliot and e. e. cummings—the first two poets I heard read, in 1959—and almost no one else. The Iowa Writers Workshop existed, but in most colleges—as in mine—if creative writing courses were given at all, they were in fiction. There was a kind of general social agreement that inwardness—and the art of inwardness, lyric poetry—was a terrain for specialists, a little unhealthy, a little feminine, at a time when "feminine" could still mean "unreal" or "second-rate." Fiction, the art of extroversion, which dealt with struggles in the world, and held out some promise of worldly success, might be presumed to be of some general interest; poetry was not. And the one younger poet everyone had heard of howled in favor of madness, homosexuality, and "super-Communism."

When did these attitudes start to change? I think popular music is an index. By 1966, the mass audience which a few years before listened only to love songs, was eager for lyrics about states of mind, long dream-journeys with or without the help of drugs, reexaminations of values, revolutionary defiance. In the ideological writers of the time—Laing, Marcuse, Paul Goodman—inwardness and political activism were associated, not contrasted as they sometimes are now. It was "Romans Angry About the Inner World," in Robert Bly's memorable phrase, who did not understand that we were bombing parts of ourselves in North Vietnam. Psychotherapy began to be perhaps the one experience that was all but universal in the educated upper middle class. And when the hope of real social change receded, it left a generation used to looking inward, and inclined to turn to psychology, and to the more psychological forms of religion, for the sense of how to live which neither God-and-country values nor revolutionary values any longer gave them. And for a smaller, but substantial, portion of that generation, the art traditionally associated with those areas of life was no longer the property of professionals alone. The changes in the institutions surrounding poetry which I have mentioned came in with the 1960s, and have never gone away.

The new audience is, as I have suggested, largely middle- and upper-middle-class. It is still more female than male, and the men tend—as in my Northern California group—to get a little extra respect; they have overcome a taboo. One effect the new audience has had on poetry, for good or bad, has surely been the continued popularity of the personal or "confessional" mode. The fashion among writers turned against it in the early 1970s; critics worried, from the beginning, that it was not "universal" enough. The audience knew that the reverse was true; and it suited their deep inclination to use poetry for the clarification of—and for wisdom about—their own intimate histories. (Though this emphasis on the personal has been criticized as apolitical, I think it is also the audience that gives political poetry the high prestige it has.

Liberal guilt—including guilt over what is perceived as the self-betrayal of the 1960s—is a powerful force with them; Carolyn Forché or Lucille Clifton will always draw bigger crowds than Robert Pinsky or Louise Glück.)

But I think the audience has had a subtler, and a far more important, effect—as, perhaps, the very existence of a substantial audience always does. It is the frequency, and skill, with which a conversational manner is now used to explore even the most earnest and meditative subjects. Yeats and Eliot had that skill, addressing the—respectively—patriotic Irish and Anglican audiences they had gained through their plays and public appearances. For American poets of the 1950s, this possibility was simply not available. Even in Robert Lowell's *Life Studies*, colloquial phrases are set in as carefully and anxiously as jewels: "adults *champing* for their ritual Friday *spin*," "Back in my *throw-away* and shaggy span / of adolescence" (italics mine). It may be objected that this was due to Lowell's temperament, or to his "academic" connections. But even in Frank O'Hara's wonderfully breezy poems, I hear a joke in the voice, directed to a small and very specific in-group: "Look, I'm talking the way we talk and calling it poetry. Isn't it fun?—like putting a toilet bowl in an art show."

Consider, by contrast, the opening lines of C. K. Williams's "My Mother's Lips":

> Until I asked her to please stop doing it and was astonished
>   to find that she not only could
> but from the moment I asked her in fact would stop doing it,
>   my mother, all through my childhood,
> when I was saying something to her, something important,
>   would move her lips as I was speaking
> so that she seemed to be saying under her breath the very
>   words I was saying as I was saying them.

Here we have, as in Frost, the poetry of the sentence—the spoken sentence, with its oblique way of thinking through things, its long suspensions and repetitions, its successful obliviousness to literary rules of conciseness. For such poetry to be written, it was necessary, first, that such sentences should be spoken often, in a culture increasingly conscious and analytic about family relationships. And secondly, I think, it was necessary that the poet have a real sense of contact with that culture—for instance, through month after month of giving readings—and a sense of what perceptions were shared and could be built on, for it to become natural to cast such delicate inner ruminations as speech. Even in a conspicuously difficult poet like Jorie Graham, it is striking how often the "Dear reader" tone occurs. "I swear to you she wanted back into the shut, the slow," one poem begins; or another—

> So Look I said this is the burning bush we're in it
>   it has three faces
>
> It's a day's work it's the hand that takes and the other one
>
> The other one the mother the one whose grief is the visible
>   world

Nor is such poetry anti-intellectual, as willfully demotic poetry tends to be. Indeed, it shows a keen sense of what level of learned allusion its audience will accept, including the fact that, as Alfred Corn writes, "at present, readers of poetry are more likely to have accurate perceptions and definite feelings about, say, the *Pastoral Symphony,* or *The Cherry Orchard,* or *The Twittering Machine,* than about the Snake River, the hornbeam tree, or the engine of a Diamond Reo."

Mind you, I am not arguing that this poetry is in any way superior to poetry written for a small audience, or in total solitude. Finally, audience has little to do with absolute literary merit. But different virtues become possible when it is there, and they deserve to be recognized.

If the present situation has drawbacks, they come from the peculiarities of an audience so many of whom aspire to be recognized as poets in their own right. When even so distinguished an elder statesman as Stanley Kunitz predicts an age when there will be "great poems," but not "great poets," we are somewhere in the neighborhood of Andy Warhol's "everyone will be a star for ten minutes." The level of journeyman poetry is in fact high, in some ways perhaps higher than it has ever been; and serious poets have a natural tendency to be kind to the special vulnerabilities of those nice people who listen so attentively to their own work. Under such circumstances, it becomes very hard to draw a clear line between work whose main value is therapeutic or inspirational and work which really addresses, and expands, the possibilities of the art itself. A not unthoughtful student of mine recently wrote me, praising a poem containing the following lines in the same terms as Philip Larkin and Sylvia Plath:

> To live in this world
>
> you must be able
> to do three things:
> to love what is mortal;
> to hold it
>
> against your bones knowing
> your own life depends on it;
> and, when the time comes to let it go,
> to let it go.

To me, this is little different from what the average self-help book would say about loss. But my student is not alone in esteeming it more highly. The author of these lines won a Pulitzer Prize for poetry. C. K. Williams has not; nor has Jorie Graham; nor have any of the poets in that age span who seem to me genuine innovators.

But enough. We are always too inclined to say the glass is half empty rather than half full. If we could recognize that it is one of the glories of our culture that the level of journeyman poetry is so high, and still draw a clear line between that and the best poetry, the Golden Age would have returned. But even as things stand, I think poets have reason to be grateful to have this audience to write for. They are, in a way, a rather noble group of people—conscious of being a minority; given to self-examination; very perceptive, especially on psychological matters. They are alert to the world around them, but want to know the old culture that the society as a

whole is so quickly forgetting. They bear the strain of apoca-
lyptic times, without falling into one of the various Fundamen-
talisms, or into mere acquisitiveness; and poetry is one of the
means they use to help them do so. In how many ages have
poets really had better listeners, if such accounts could ever be
fairly drawn?

Stories about the Self (I)

It might be that, for a literary historian from the future, the most interesting technical development in American poetry in the last two decades of this century would be the refinement of (largely autobiographical) narrative. It would be a little surprising, since "confessional poetry"—almost from the moment that unfortunate term was coined—has been the whipping boy of half a dozen newer schools, New Surrealism, New Formalism, Language poetry. Yet it has remained the staple of what comes near to being poetry's mass audience—the earnest beginners, in small cities, on college campuses of all kinds and sizes, for whom poetry is a way of setting their lives in order. On the more sophisticated level, all the negative attention may well have stimulated poets to approach the self's story with a tact, a self-awareness, an eye to exclusions and thematic "figure in the carpet," fiction writers have taken for granted for generations (think of *To the Lighthouse*, "Prelude," *A Portrait of the Artist as a Young Man*). One reads the best of the newer narrative poetry with a sense of point of view, of strategic timing and delayed exposition, that makes even the great poems of Lowell and Plath feel like raw lyric by comparison.

Yet I wouldn't entirely agree with Alan Shapiro's sense, in a fascinating recent essay ("In Praise of the Impure: Narrative Consciousness in Poetry," *Triquarterly* 81 [spring–summer 1991]), that recent narrative poetry, being more social, is in reaction against the concentrated interior moment not only in High Modernism but even in Lowell and Ginsberg. That seems to me too absolute an either-or; from another

American Poetry Review 22, no. 2 (March–April 1993).

point of view, all three could be seen as instants along the same vector, an extension of Pound's "the natural object is always the adequate symbol." Heaven knows few poets are working in High Modernist modes at the moment; but some of those who are—Peter Dale Scott, for instance—have made significant contributions, by their very ellipses, to the art of storytelling.

I've spoken of fiction as a model; but it may be useful to notice two other, opposite models, both a little beyond the spectrum of the fictional. One would be movies, which explain nothing, but convey both interpretation and feeling-tone by a series of immensely subtle visual and spatial cues. The other would be the essay, which does nothing but explain, but has a freedom to switch anecdotal subject, setting, and mode of address allowed to almost no other genre. Movies are a model for poetry—as for fiction and so much else—simply because they are our culture's most popular, and most technically inventive, mode of storytelling. Essays may have become a model because of the heated discussion surrounding the term *discursive* after the publication of Robert Pinsky's influential and controversial book *The Situation of Poetry.* (Indeed, Shapiro's sense of a *new* narrative school might be brought into sharper focus by calling it an essayistic school.)

One could trace this mode back to the poets who have most shaped it, poets like Pinsky, C. K. Williams, Frank Bidart. But I'd prefer, in this essay, and the succeeding one, to look at the mostly younger poets who have been able to take the mode for granted, and have brought to it a new finesse, variation, assurance. The title poem of Alan Shapiro's own new volume, *Covenant,* is a spectacular instance of the interweaving of fictional, essayistic, and cinematic possibilities. (I'll concede, at the start, that I have no reason to consider this poem "confessional," other than the similarity of atmosphere to certain poems that are explicitly about the poet's own family.) "Covenant" tells the story of a Jewish family reunion from the terrible perspective of the "youngest sister" 's death "three months away." We know from fairly early on that she will die, but it takes us most of the length of the poem, and many hints, to learn exactly what happens. (Affected, either mentally or physically, by a stroke, she drops a lighted cigarette and sets herself on fire.) But the focus of the poem, while this appalling story is being postponed, is on the inner violence within the family, the tensions around food, around giving and taking, control, intrusion, and contamination. "The oldest sister, her two hands on the table, / about to push herself up," waits grimly while the others go on talking,

> Her gaze so tense with purpose she can almost
> see germs spawning in the mess of white fish
> flaking from the spines, the smear of egg yolk
> and the torn rolls disfiguring the china;
> as if the meal, the moment it is over,
> the meal she made a point of telling them
> she shopped for, got up early to prepare,
> were now inedible, because uneaten.

The long sentence unwinds down through the lines, with a muscular effort that imitates the work of arriving at, and formulating, a psychological insight, as well as the tense insistences of the sister's own harangue. And from the middle of this sentence the horrid, unforgettable visual details flash out—this much, at least, has been learned from the revolt against imagism—with an off-guard vividness they could never have had if the poet's main, declared intent had been to *describe*.

Shapiro is usually a formal poet, but aggressively not a New Formalist. The difference lies between the little lick of self-conscious pseudo-elegance that tends to get laid down on every line when form is an end in itself, and the immense variety of tones it can take, uses it can serve, in the hands of a poet whose eye is on something more serious. At one extreme, there's the puzzled, driving, working-things-out Larkinesque kind of line we've just heard; at the other, the Frostian syncopated line that catches the lilt of colloquial speech by setting it against a metrical expectation. "Listen, she would be saying, listen, Charlie"; "What can you do? What are ya gonna do?" A great deal of Shapiro's poem is taken up with capturing, in pentameter, certain Jewish-American storytelling mannerisms and the emotions they reveal—bewilderment, pain, self-importance, the triumph over experience by reenacting it—more or less the same range of reactions to human misfortune caught by that famous "Yes" in Elizabeth Bishop's "The Moose," a poem Shapiro has written about eloquently.

All of this imitation, and examination, of storytelling reaches its horrid fruition when we finally hear the story of the youngest sister's death in the older sister's voice:

> And selfish. She was selfish, that one. After
> all those years of living with that bum,
> her husband, may his cheap soul rest in peace,
> didn't *she* deserve a little pleasure?
> And anyway, what could be done for her?
> Didn't the stroke just make it easier
> for her to sit all day, and smoke, and not care
> ashes were falling on the couch, the carpet;
> her bathrobe filthy, filthy?

It sounds like the worst Jewish-mother joke one has ever heard: the youngest sister, it would seem, has died just to burden the older sister's life more, to "[sit] there, / the queen of Sheba," establishing that "*she* was there, *she* was always there, / her big sister, to clean up the mess."

Yet at this very moment of grotesque satire, Shapiro's essayistic, explanatory tone comes in to move the poem toward the lyrical, and toward compassion. The bad mother becomes the child, her hostility her way of defending herself against guilt, helplessness, and self-reproach:

> and now they will hear the old unfairnesses,
> old feuds and resentments come to her voice
> like consolation, like a mother helping
> her recite the story of that bad last day—
> all that smoke, and running in with nothing
> but the dishtowel to beat down the flames

What seems to me cinematic in the poem is the way light and temperature function throughout, both as a foreshadowing— or a reminder—of the youngest sister's unspeakable fate, and as a subtler emotional index of the "wavering frail zone it" ("the body," but, by extension, the ego and its anxieties) "needs / to be forgotten." Early in the poem "sunlight" is "only just now *catching* on / a corner of the window" (italics mine); later it "burns brick by brick all morning toward the window / like a slow fuse"; until finally

> the sun has only just now
> caught in the window, and its bright plaque warms
> the air so gradually that none of them
> can know it's warming, or that soon someone,
> distracted by a faint sheen prickling the skin,
> will break the story, look up toward the window
> and, startled by the full glare, check the time.

What saves this from being gimmicky is partly that this last, most brilliant recurrence comes after the flash-forward to the death narrative; and partly that it so profoundly encapsulates the deepest issues in the poem. The "figure in the carpet" is "the harm that's imperceptibly / but surely coming for them," time itself, the unnoticed flowering of causes and possibilities, always at once too slow and too quick for our attention. On the psychological level, *control* is the theme the poem settles on, the impossible wish that makes the claustrophobic atmosphere of this family comprehensible, even as it also provides an avenue for its aggressions:

> Nothing bad, right now, can happen here
> except as news, bad news the brother and sister
> mull and rehearse, puzzle and fret until
> it seems the very telling of it is
> what keeps them safe. And safe, too, the oldest sister. . . .
> dreaming of how the soapsuds curdle and slide
> over the dishes in a soothing fury,
> not minding that it scalds her hands to hold
> each plate and cup and bowl under the hot,
> hard jet of water, if it gets them clean.

Temperature, again. What a savage ending it is—as if the self-punishing energy in the family became the fire that burns the sister alive. And yet a compassionate ending, in its willingness to enter, identify with, and *explain* the labyrinth of motive.

I've loved Shapiro's work—its Larkinesque measures, its truthfulness—ever since *Happy Hour,* an interrogation of the psychology of love as severe, in its way, as Proust's. This new book is immensely richer and more varied, turning on our covenants with God and fate as well as the grimmer, pettier trade-offs within the family. It will please different readers in different ways. Some, I know, are most taken with the Milos-zian poems on historical irony, commonplaceness, and terror. My own favorites, aside from "Covenant," are "The Lesson" and the series on marriage and fatherhood running, approxi-mately, from "Owl" through "Separation of the Waters." The former takes up the explosive theme of child sexual abuse without self-pity, concentrating instead on the glamour the pedophile is able to conjure up for the group of boys. The latter are *healthy*—as the great marriage sequences in recent memory emphatically are not—and for that reason all the more devastating in their sense of the daily bargain with fate.

Tom Sleigh's poem "Fish Story," like "Covenant," has un-speakable violence and pain, slowly disclosed, as its core sub-ject. I take it up as a much clearer instance of the essayistic way of organizing a poem, its oddities and its advantages. (Sleigh's book, like Shapiro's, appears in the University of Chicago Press's Phoenix Poets series, which also publishes Lloyd Schwartz and Anne Winters, among others. The series deserves praise for having identified itself, more than any other publisher, with the best of newer narrative work.)

"Fish Story" begins, in the unapologetically intellectual way Frank Bidart's work, more than anyone else's, has made think-able to younger writers,

> I was reading *Plutarch's Lives,* about the gods,
> When I remembered someone I once knew, who came to our
>   home
> On Sundays for dinner with his girlfriend Kay

The leap, of course, is anything but accidental. The work of the poem will be to define, through this "someone," what the gods who "come down to us disguised" would be like. At first, the definition seems heroic and uncomplicated, if a little hackneyed. The man, a fisherman, a contrast to Kay's gay ex-boyfriend, is superhuman in his appetites and strength, if also in killing; he talks about

> How the deck gets slimy with scales,
> And the sixteen-ounce steaks you eat morning, noon, and
>   night,
> And how you need that kind of nourishment
>
> To gaff hundreds of fish and club them to death

"A fish story," the speaker thinks, when the man shows his "Blood-soaked socks"; but later, when he himself is seized with the archetypal adolescent ambition of running away to sea, those socks become enviable, the "badge or token / That I was more than what I seemed," and finally "As much an emblem as a thunderbolt or trident." But the moment the theme of divinity is finally, explicitly articulated, it takes a darker turn—an unlikeness to, perhaps even a deficiency in, human consciousness:

> So that sometimes I wonder if he himself
>
> Weren't a kind of god: He had the face
> Of a sleepy animal, heavy lids and bushy hair and his eyes
> Went blind when he talked, his spoon hesitating
>
> Halfway to his mouth and the steam
> Off the soup curling upward in the sunlight.
> He talked about the death penalty as a good thing

And here, with wonderful black comic timing, the poem releases its thunderbolt—

> Which seems strange considering what later happened:
> He was separated from his wife, with two kids,
> When he'd met Kay, and one night, with a flensing knife,
>
> He stabbed his wife twenty-seven times,
> Face, throat, chest, back, stabbed her even in the eye
> Like Marlowe.

(I sometimes wonder what future readers will make of such ostentatiously "literary" effects as "Like Marlowe." For us, I think, they depend on the presumption that violence is so commonplace in the news and popular culture that we need to come on it out of context—in literary history, for instance—to feel how odd, and how nauseatingly real, it is.)

The murder makes the man even more mysterious, for he seems to have committed it in a kind of trance, and gets off with "A temporary insanity plea, which I admit / Seems accurate." In confronting this, the poem returns to the mythic; and, I would add, to the essayist's freedom not only of subject matter but of tone, since "poetic temperaments" are not expected to be so impressive and so skeptical in the same breath:

> I see him like that, straight-backed in his chair,
> Stone-faced as Ephesian Diana, her throat encircled
>
> By a necklace of bull's testicles, what poetic temperaments
> Mistake for breasts!

The stakes are high here, for all the cynicism. Is the divine grand and nourishing (the man's "hand . . . seemed gentle and faithful that Sunday"); or is it a rigid atavistic stupidity? From this image the poem cuts directly to its second *coup de theatre*:

>   —I think of him at their wedding
> Staring straight into Kay's eyes and her saying, "I do,"
>
> The flashbulbs gasping in the startled air
> And the air holding still as they drag out the kiss,
> And then his hand clasped over hers on the cake knife.

Like Shapiro's last line, this one makes us wince, taking us straight back to the unspeakable crime. Yet the tenderness in it all but overrides that, leaving us, again, with questions. Are human beings dupes—rabbits mesmerized by the snake—or do they discover unbelievably trustworthy powers in themselves, when they fall in love with the ambiguous gods? The slightly heightened tone of the writing—permitted, one feels, by "Ephesian Diana," for all the undercutting—reinforces this double-edged sense of awe, leaving us a little "startled," like the "air." (Not less so, perhaps, because that phrase echoes a classical scene in Rilke's First Elegy.)

Reading this poem leaves me feeling heartened, not only about Sleigh's own development (it seems to me the best single poem in *Waking,* though others have even more overpowering subjects), but about the possibilities in contemporary writing it typifies. There's so much more amplitude, of experience and tone, than in the Deep Image style of twenty years ago, the New Critical style of forty. *Pace* Shapiro, it even seems closer to the excitement of Modernism, though the means are utterly different. Certainly many unfortunate prejudices have had to be overcome to get to it: that intellect and learned reference are incompatible with emotion; that a speech-based style cannot go with the numinous, or either with any vestige of the formal line. (Sleigh's poem has a much more relaxed metric than Shapiro's, but consider "The flashbulbs gasping in the startled air.") It suggests that we live at a flexible, omnivorous moment in the history of American poetry; and however much discouragingly unambitious work is also out there, that is something to be grateful for.

Stories about the Self (II)

There is a quotation from Willa Cather that, for all its old-fashioned ring, has haunted me ever since I first came on it:

> If the writer achieves anything noble, anything enduring, it must be by giving himself absolutely to his material. He fades away into the land and people of his heart; he dies of love only to be born again.

It reminds me of a passage Gary Snyder is fond of quoting, from the thirteenth-century Zen master Dogen:

> To carry yourself forward and experience myriad things is delusion. But myriad things coming forth and experiencing *themselves* is awakening.

On the face of it, both quotations would seem to be utterly against the idea of personal art. Read carefully, I think both acknowledge that—as the object relations theorist Christopher Bollas has suggested—the self exists hidden within the objects it has cherished, to be resurrected there, in Cather's terms, or awakened, in Dogen's, in a flexible plenitude sometimes lost when we try to examine the self as if it were a fixed object. Another translation of the Dogen passage reads: "Acting on and witnessing oneself in the advent of myriad things is enlightenment."

I think we all know intuitively what goes wrong in art when the self goes out to the myriad things like a conquering army,

American Poetry Review 22, no. 5 (September–October 1993).

trying to make them express it (though we might differ enormously as to just which poets and fictionists most embody this failing). Recently, reading the *New York Times Book Review*, I saw someone praised as "the most talented American poet under the age of forty" for lines like the following:

> Now in a gilded apse the celestial globe
> Has rolled to the end of an invisible rope
> And come to rest on a cliff in a blue-green garden.
> I look up, as if nothing had killed my hope,
> At a blue sphere, buoyant in the sixth-century tides
> Still surging and dying away through San Vitale,
> Where a spring has glinted in the numinous
> Fresh-cut grass for more than a millennium.

Now I have nothing against touristic poems about Europe, having written a number of them myself. But how nakedly this one seems to value the cultural objects simply for being cultural objects, able to make things "numinous"! And how it all serves as backdrop for the more than Victorian self-pity of "I look up, as if nothing had killed my hope"—which, one can't help feeling, the poet would have had a harder time bringing off stuck, as Whitman wished us, back among the kitchenware. To me it is a little example of how poetry can deaden the "myriad things," by forcing them into too willed and self-centered a design.

In the last few years I've been struck by a number of poems that, by contrast, simply open themselves, in a lovely, leisurely way, to the world of the poet's affections (usually, but not always, the world of childhood). Only slowly and by inference do we discover that they are also about the making of a poet's mind, or the survival of some crisis—stories about the self. It seems part of the same flowering-out, by experiment and variation, of the possibilities of the personal, that I discussed in my previous essay.

"The Reservoir" is the longest poem in Debra Allbery's *Walking Distance,* the 1990 winner of the University of Pittsburgh Press's Starrett Prize, and a book that would certainly be on my mind if I were doing anything so rash as ranking poets under forty. It is an honest and original chapter in the long history of the love-hate relation between middle America and its artist children. The town Allbery calls Enterprise, Ohio, was also the model for Sherwood Anderson's Winesburg. (When that book came out, it was burned in the public square; now the city limits signs say "(Winesburg)," just as, south of Chartres in the Ile-de-France, one can visit a town called Illiers-Combray.)

"The Reservoir" begins by confessing that the poet's return home, to two comically onerous summer jobs, is partly psychic retreat—"deep habit, no danger"—and partly a never-relinquished hope that "some of the endings she needed / might be found, after all, in Enterprise, Ohio." The sights and sounds of the place are emblems of what Thoreau called "quiet desperation," and at the same time so deeply messages to the poet's own self-questioning that there is no escaping the human commonality:

> Walking, she passes these signs
> all summer—one is painted in red
> on a ripped bed sheet and hangs
> from an upstairs window:
> "You've had it? *You're* the problem!"
> And this hand-printed and taped
> to someone's front door: "Day Sleeper."
> In the Christian bookstore window,
> a white-on-black placard: "Does mortality
> limit you?"

The receptiveness of this poem to its world is easier to experience than to describe. It is stalled and beautiful at once, depressed and full of affection, like the small-town summer. The poem could easily seem too long, but somehow doesn't. The severely objectifying third-person alternates with first-person passages in italics, yielding to a dreamlike, merged perspective the rest of the poem resists:

> *Trains passed through like they were still important*
> *and I'd stand in their wind, reading the flaking names*
> *on old boxcars,* Eric Lackawanna. Chessie, Rock Island.

> *After they passed, the quiet went deeper,*
> *the land lay light green after green, almost seamless.*

Real dreams, by contrast, are reminders of crisis, psychic danger, the need for change, "the sky of Enterprise filled / with tornadoes, with colored balloons." Brief scenes with her mother, high school classmates, an old boyfriend about to get married—

> the exclusiveness,
> the strange gravity, of his "we,"
> how it tops her halting "I's"
> the way paper-covers-rock

—edge her out of her sense of really belonging, but not out of the sense that,

> like anyone,
> it's belonging she wants, it's the idea
> of *settled* or *permanent address.*
> And all she's done has been only so much
> rent paid toward that place.

Most of the high lyric moments in the poem are associated with the reservoir of the title, just outside of town, where "she" goes running. It becomes the vehicle of the wish to be inside and outside at once, the peculiar kind of distance (implicitly, the distance of art) that permits love and hate to be held in balance:

> And alongside her, beer cans,
> rubbers, torn cardboard, bleached crawdads,
> and she runs it again and everyday, for it's only
> from this height and pace she can love her town.

(And here I think we can see how Allbery, like Alan Shapiro, is quietly one of the most inventive of contemporary metrists. That last line *counts* as iambic pentameter; but it sings as a half-anapestic tetrameter, the very momentum that glides above the world of counted things: "from this height and pace she can love her town." Never rigidly bound by meter, but tending to return to it at the high points, Allbery restores the relation to speech, to thinking-things-through, it had in Frost and Jarrell.)

The poem returns to the reservoir at the end, when the playing back and forth between the speaker's sense of superiority and inferiority to her given world, the wish for "distances . . . to try alone" and the wish for "belonging," have brought it to a point of crisis:

> She's outside of Enterprise, running the reservoir,
> singing to herself *The water is wide,*
> looking past the south and east edges
> of town, at the reach of August sky
> and black clouds moving quickly
> from the west, and she's thinking
> *Sometimes if I open my eyes very wide*
> *there's this space which is like*
> *room for error. And I see limits,*
> *I see things that can change my mind.*

Rather wonderfully, the poem finds wisdom not on either side of its dichotomies, but rather in the psychic transaction that leaves both available as agencies of change. And the ending seems to me equally wonderful. The poem, which up to this point has found ingenious ways of subordinating narrative to catalog, concludes with a baldly unmediated anecdote:

> Long ago, a teacher had told her
> about his genius friend, and how
> he'd sit with his thoughts wherever
> they came to him, thinking them through,
> and how he found him once, drenched,
> oblivious, sitting chin-in-hands
> on a street corner. And this
> was the first ambition she could remember,
> to not have sense enough to come in out of the rain.

It is a delicately humorous acknowledgment of how the poet has come to overvalue the outside perspective; the self-destructive potential of that; and at the same time the real value of inner distance, of activities that are their own reason for being, of all that goes outside the bounds of small-town common sense. It's one of the most brilliant and charming instances of seemingly suspended closure I know of in recent poetry.

"The Reservoir" makes sparing but skillful use of a musical organization by motif, so that we hear more of *You've had it? You're the problem!, The water is wide,* and other key phrases as the crisis approaches. Such organization may well be a necessity when divagatoriness, rather than plot, is the form the love of place cries out for. In Jeanne Foster's "The Pearl River" (published under her earlier writing name, Jeanne Foster Hill, in *The Hudson Review,* summer 1985), it is carried to a level more musical than traditionally poetic. The initial notes have to do with fear of the world, reassurance, and then discovering the limits of the knowableness, the reassurance, of anything outside the self:

> This little finger, she reassured,
> rolling the baseball-stunned knuckle
> of the child's left little finger between her padded thumb
> and forefinger, couldn't be broken.
> It is so limber, it could be bent
> like a sapling under weight of snow to earth
> and not snap.
> . . . .
> She is as doe to fawn,
> that teacher, who only once
> became enraged and broke
> the scissors against the desk. The little girl sat
> amazed.
>
> But fingers . . .
> I've said what I could say
> about them.

Against the background of these issues the world of childhood exfoliates. On the one hand, the child's fear, as in Elizabeth Bishop's "In the Waiting Room," of all she is exposed to, made part of, simply by existing—

> She in her blue pinafore, trimmed with tiny red and yellow
> flowers and green leaves, was afraid
> of the very cousins—the red-haired Jim
> and the green-eyed Barbara and their hairy friend

—and, even more, of the intimations of death, cruelty, the ultimate indifference of things, her uncle beheading a hen and the body "run(ning) headless under the calm, observant gaze / of the loblolly pines." And on the other hand, the childhood sense of things being simultaneous with their meaning and that meaning, always, intimately related to herself:

> And the house was watched over,
> its silver-tin roof shooting light from the sun
> into the very hearts of those pines.

Certain leitmotif phrases, repeated and varied throughout the poem, dramatize the tension of these antinomies. "Nothing would let go"—the sense of trauma, invasion, contamination—plays against the more problematic "Nothing was simply let go," which carries a certain painful promise for the speaker as artist, as therapeutic self-discoverer, as an adult frightened of the total loss of the past, the speaker who will eventually transmute the phrase into

> Everything is kept, but nothing
> is easily recovered.

Another leitmotif phrase is "The Pearl River, the dividing line." Its literal meaning is geographical—between Louisiana and Mississippi—but since the poem nowhere mentions this fact, the reader is left to imagine other borders, conscious and unconscious, childhood and adulthood, life and death. At first the river seems a kind of dream river, something like the collective unconscious, which the child approaches through the back of a closet, like the magic land in C. S. Lewis's *The Lion, the Witch, and the Wardrobe*. Images of mirroring, recognition, condensations, and simultaneities reinforce this feeling. (The psychoanalyst Hans Loewald suggested that condensation is one of the qualities that distinguish unconscious imagi-

native thinking from rational thinking.) The river is both it-
self a sign and inscribed with signs, of threats, of dangerous
vitality:

> The Pearl River, the dividing line,
> winds like a water moccasin through the red clay soil.
> The moon turns its full face toward
> the upward turned face, and the river shines
> like pearl. Upon its surface
> a water moccasin carves the shape
> of a worker's scythe.

The river is, perhaps most important, the place where "The
song" is first heard, a song reconciling the opposed principles
of nourishment and threat, value, trauma, and sexual muck:

> Kept all these years,
> a treasure watched over by the pirate's ghost,
> the pearl in the oyster growing in a bed of mud,
> the milk before it is milked from the fangs . . .

The scene, as it is repeated, is very delicately inscribed with
the sexual and racial tensions common to Southern writing.
The original singer of the song is a "black man"; it is his
"upward turned face / shining like black silver," and not just
the river's, that the moon mirrors. And the hidden spectator
of this otherness is at once furtive child and the idealized
image of Southern womanhood, restrained by her protection:

> A shadow
> white as a madonna lily moves away
> under the dark green cloaks of our forefathers,
> the loblolly pines.

In acknowledging these meanings, and in making the song
her own, able "to recall itself / from the labyrinth," the
speaker becomes adult: "A slender woman walks out the other
side / into daylight."
    In the second half of the poem, the adult half, nearly every
incident, every phrase, is repeated from the first half—the

ego being, in Freud's words, where the id has been. Some of the discoveries are hilarious—

> Uncle Al laid down the hatchet.
> The green-eyed Barbara, the red-haired Jim,
> and Harry, their friend, stood around and watched

—where we realize that the child has misheard the world in the image of the terror and animality already there in her unconscious: "their hairy friend." In the last section, a slightly hostile, challenging blackface voice keeps asking "Is it you, girl?" and the question seems addressed to all the elements in the scene: the hiding shadow, the woman who "walks out the other side," the river itself, shining and reflecting—as if only when all of these larger and smaller selves are acknowledged, will selfhood be whole. Yet the poem never makes this too easy; the adult speaker who can offer the words of consolation to herself remains somehow melancholy in her protectiveness, and the poem ends on the last notes of its overture, the note of muteness, of reaching the limits of the comprehensible:

> Young things are so fragile, she whispers
> and remembers the teacher who stroked the knuckle of her
>   left
> little finger. Only once did she become enraged
> and break the scissors against the desk.
>
> But fingers . . .
> I've said what I could say
> about them.

Brenda Hillman's "Canyon," from her book *Fortress,* is also a story about a landscape. It's about a park, just outside a city, half wild, half tame, with its "Jewel Lake" and its ducks, but also the high bare slopes, drier, more ignitable as summer goes on, that seem an intimation that "the normal soul / has an extra soul above it." It is a story about feeling, like the landscape, on the edge of ultimates; small and uncertain in that exposure, yet the vehicle of energies at once mystical and mischievous—

> Two fawns in the sun: twin deaths: one
> gazes with unbearable steadiness;
> the other looks up as the id looks up,
> his ears twitching the victory sign

Perhaps it is about a relationship suffused with these quali-
ties—but an impeded relationship, whose obstacles and sepa-
rations may be the occasion for the solitary wanderings in the
park ("I pretended / you were living in another country, not
far, / yet impossible to reach. . . . / and I had rushed out here /
to be your opposite").

In some ways, the poem talks most powerfully about love
by talking about perception. Both have the power to give
access to that realm of the "extra soul," where "you are known
completely / by seeing, known as if by a secret companion."
Both, too, are problematic. In the structure of the poem, the
merged immediacy of this particular relationship—

> Thinking I'd feel nothing
> without your hands, their girlish strength (as you
> could feel nothing without my boyish ones)

—is to the work of doubt, tyrannical expectation, finding out
who the other person really is, how much meshing is possible
(how can it be avoided, one protests, when two people think of
making a life together?) as the spider that

> is neither subject nor object, it has no separate
> motions in its realm but lets itself gently down
> into the notch and crack of the inexpressible

is to the birdwatcher who hasn't really seen the bird until he
can name it ("oriole"); is to the breakdowns we can make, like
Zeno's paradox of the arrow, out of our own "flash" of seeing:

> I recall the illustration in the text, how the solitary
> impulse, like a hiker, hurried down,
>
> disturbed the obstinate whiteness
> of the membrane, climbed

into blockish boats ("receptors"),
was ferried across the synapse, the little

Lethe between two cells.

No less than doubt, the desire to control the outcome is an almost overwhelming force that landscape must absorb, and eventually alter, in this poem. The fear of loss—loss of the dream, and of the immediate experience, of oneness, no less than loss of each other—almost breaks the psyche, and the bare hills, with the "clarity" of their "lacunae," have their own way of embodying the absoluteness of this claim. Yet the lesson of nature—the hills drying out, the season moving toward autumn—is that things must change, and with change there is always some degree of loss: "the light was changing, and would not change back." Against this, the very divagatoriness of the poem is a kind of defenseless defense. An enactment of the immense creativity, and the stasis, of obsessive love, it prepares for the poem's eventual assent to valuing experience over certainty:

> I can't look too closely at the faces
> of runners; they wear their deaths,
> working out for the long, local races,
> or when they descend the haunted road
>
> after the natural morphine makes of the body
> a stem of soothing light
> . . . .
> I think about the woman in the cap
> who needed water, who staggered like a drunk,
> for whom the cheering didn't matter; she said
>
> she didn't know the difference
> between the men in lab coats and the finish line,
> but with great yearning,
> she spoke of the race as of a beloved tormentor.

Yet it is one of the great strengths of the poem that it never chooses between the "reality" of love and a more disillusioned, or more resignedly experiential, perspective. Instead, after a troubled, inconclusive encounter—the "you," always represented as the more rational, and the more anxious, of the two, sinks into "gloom," and "this mild calm is not the happiness we envisioned"—the poem returns to the image of the fawns:

> We shall know without judgment
> in the fullness of time—it says that
> in some religion. The brave fawn waits
> for its companion, and its spots shine
>
> like spilled quarters in the sun.
> The scared one steps into the road at last,
> becomes the other one;
> then the spotted earth becomes the fawn's back.

It's a wonderful summary of all the tensions and hopes, braveries and hesitations, in the poem (the "spilled quarters" refer to a pay phone call, earlier). The last lines—the protective coloration—are at once an affirmation of twinship, both between the lovers and between perception and the world, and a way of leaving open the question whether it can be lived out, short of apocalypse, death, becoming the earth.

What I like best, almost, in these three very lovely, structurally inventive poems, is the happy absence of competition between the "myriad things" and introspection. Enterprise, Ohio, the Pearl River, Tilden Park "com(e) forth and experienc(e) *themselves*" in these poems; they remain permanent imaginative landscapes for the reader. Yet they also cause, and/or become equivalents for, very subtly delineated states of feeling and being, states "known completely / by seeing," in Hillman's phrase. Given Dogen's concern with "awakening," perhaps it's no accident that these are poems of self-education as well as self-expression. Landscape, in them, seems to have the power to alter *every* easy, or anxious, or one-sided assessment of reality simply by standing in the face of it. And the selves that emerge at the ends of these poems seem more flexible, more tolerant of contradiction, less anxious about outcomes; surrounded, even, with the aura of a larger, more impersonal creative selfhood, like Foster's river and upturned face.

These poems also interest me intensely as a moment in the

history of genres. There are precedents, of course, certainly among the Romantics—"Frost at Midnight" comes to mind— and among Modernist long poems like *Four Quartets*. But in our own time the "confessional" poem has been so distinct, and embattled, a genre that landscape meditation has tended to hold off, in distant sectors of the map of styles. The interpenetration of their methods is a subtilizing process for both; and one more reason to be glad of the ways American poets have stuck with the personal, the last twenty years.

Eloquence and "Mere Life": A Sense of Generation

I

It is always difficult, and a little embarrassing, to write about the poetry of one's own moment—especially poetry that parallels, or has forwarded, one's own intentions as a writer. The difficulty only becomes more visible if one is asked—as I recently was—to talk about such work under the rubric *postmodern.* The word itself has a frenzied, apocalyptic ring to it. Every age, up until this one, has meant itself by the word *modern;* what kind of writing, or living, is possible when the modern is already past? Surely it must be at once extreme and artificial, inventing all the more flagrantly and self-consciously out of the fear that invention is no longer possible, in something like Wallace Stevens's

> embrace between one desperate clod
> And another in a fantastic consciousness,
> In a queer assertion of humanity

There is built into the word postmodern a prejudice in favor of all avant-gardes of self-consciousness, and against writing that assumes a constancy and depth in our feelings about some of the objects that have always been there—lovers, friends, parents and children, landscape, the contemplative dimension.

Poetry Flash, May 1986.

Still, our times *are* different from other times, in ways too familiar, terrible, and tragicomic to need repeating; and some of our best writing is bound, even when drawing on age-old currents of feeling, to add something new and strange. A case in point is Louise Glück's retelling of the first chapters of *Genesis* under the very different biblical title "Lamentations." I quote the opening lines:

> They were both still,
> the woman mournful, the man
> branching into her body.
>
> But god was watching.
> They felt his gold eye
> projecting flowers on the landscape.
>
> Who knew what he wanted?
> He was god, and a monster.
> So they waited. And the world
> filled with his radiance,
> as though he wanted to be understood.

Consider the image of god's "gold eye / projecting flowers on the landscape." It makes one think of the fine work with gold in early Renaissance paintings—a very traditional kind of aesthetic pleasure, and a traditional vision of the freshness of the world as it issues from God's hand. And yet, the modern overtones of the word "projecting"—a movie projector, and Freudian "projection"—move us toward the next stanza's paranoid and claustrophobic feeling about being imposed on by an alien consciousness, even an alien "radiance." I am reminded of R. D. Laing's story of the patient who dreams that his life is being dreamed by a sleeping giant, and then is terrified that he will be annihilated when the giant wakes up. The fear of God in its old sense—a fear of what God may do—is replaced, or augmented, by the peculiarly contemporary fear of one's own insubstantiality, and therefore of existing in other minds.

To take another example, from the third section of the poem: "Against the black sky / they saw the massive argument of light." This line, for me, takes much of its force from an echo of a line in Meredith's "Lucifer by Starlight"—already parodied once by T. S. Eliot—in which Lucifer's revolt is confuted by the immutable order of the stars, "The army of unalterable law." But in Glück's poem, the rejecting stars, seen by the fallen Adam and Eve, are not an "army" but an "argument." This is not merely religious skepticism, but the skepticism of a late twentieth-century mind that has read the Deconstructionists, and suspects that what symbols have behind them may not be vision but "massive" heavy-handed will, like the will of a god who creates the universe out of a childish feeling that no one understands him well enough. And yet, this skepticism is a lonely one. It goes with the poem's image of Adam and Eve as teenage parents, panicked by the realization of their own exclusive "authority" which their child's helplessness brings home to them—a child who (as we know, though they do not) will be so badly brought up as to become the first murderer.

What I am trying to point out is how the poem interleaves peculiarly contemporary experiences of the pain and separation inherent in being, with the experience of those things that has been there, for every generation, in the story itself. The sadness of sexual relations is a permanent element, surely. But how much feminist, as well as psychoanalytic, thinking has gone into this poem's image of the man (whether Adam or god) hoping for some completion by "branching" into another body; the woman seeing beyond this into a "mournful" emptiness, and (in a later section) grieving for the self-division created both by the overwhelming biological usefulness of her body, and by the man's image of that body.

But I don't want to suggest that the poem is a kind of machine for imposing further ironies on an already heavily ironized subject. The emotions of the poem—the emotions about men and women, and the helplessness before a terror that is also beauty—are far too intimate and insistent for that. And the voice, for all its terrified hush, has a gritty personal note to it, mockingly echoing psychobabble ("as though he wanted to be understood"), dropping into the cadences of Jewish humor ("He was god, and a monster").

Finally, the poem gathers to a kind of contemporary myth

of the origins of consciousness in the painful separations of language and sexuality:

> Nor could they keep their eyes
> from the white flesh
> on which wounds would show clearly
> like words on a page.

> And from the meaningless browns and greens
> at last God arose, His great shadow
> darkening the sleeping bodies of His children,
> and leapt into heaven.

With this change, "god" becomes "God," and human life is permanently "darkened" with the Jungian "shadow" to which the ideal of pure consciousness reduces all that it cannot assimilate. And yet, pure consciousness brings its own wonder and joy, a joy proudly rendered in terms only our century has had available:

> How beautiful it must have been,
> the earth, that first time
> seen from the air.

This poem leaves one with the heartening feeling that there is no theme too high, or rhetoric too traditional, for a poet to make contemporary and real, provided it is done with the right mixture of arrogance and delicate reserve.

II

Louise Glück's poem moves me so much partly because, from the time I began to write, I aspired to a poetry that would keep the high radiance—radiance meaning both illumination and beauty—I found in my favorite poems from the past, and yet seem to belong—and be intellectually adequate—to the present. The first half of this aspiration seemed a very lonely one, amid the tremendous prestige accorded the demotic, the spontaneous, the unhierarchical, in the late 1960s. It has been one of the consolations of growing older in the art to find out how many companions I actually had in my double ambition. Here, for instance, is Alfred Corn describing his own beginnings in *Notes from a Child of Paradise:*

> Prowling the bookstores
> And finding no epigones of Baudelaire,
> I wondered whether someone might not still—.

I take Baudelaire here as a synecdoche for what I meant by "high radiance," in all its implications—intensity, ultimate issues, music, sensuousness, intelligence. (My synecdoche would have been Rimbaud, or Hart Crane.) And yet, as Corn confesses a few lines later, when he tried the direct approach to the problem—seeing his wife across the room as Jeanne Duval with her cat—he found his work tongue-tied, artificial, false. (I found the same, when I tried to write like Crane.)

I don't know what contemporary models, or half-models, Corn found to steer him around this impasse. For me, one possible direction was represented by my teacher, Robert Lowell, and the poets commonly grouped with him, Berryman and Plath. Lowell could be quite indifferent, even hostile, to the Symbolist kind of beauty and inwardness. But grandeur, music, intelligence, cultural reach he certainly had; and the fact that he had set all these things down amid the kitchenware, in the New York (or Chicago) apartments where I too had heard "the lonely metal breathe / and gurgle like the sick," made him a hypnotically attractive model.

The other available model, for me, was the then-emerging school of Bly, Wright, Kinnell, and Merwin. These poets claimed to include everything that Lowell left out: to make it possible again to cultivate beauty without embarrassment; to treat of a beauty and terror that went beyond their occasions on the surface of life, that the ancients would have considered the voice of a god. Unlike some of my contemporaries, I never felt that this was a misguided subject; it had been, in large measure, Crane's subject, and Rilke's, and Baudelaire's. And yet, the "American surrealists," by their exclusive emphasis on the visual image, seemed to relinquish too much of the emotional, as well as intellectual, force that lay buried in the physicality of words, syntax, cadence. There was a paradox here. In their content, poems like Lowell's "Waking Early Sunday Morning" and Plath's "Ariel" spoke of a hemmed-in self, seeing through itself too clearly to imagine any satisfactory release except death. Yet it was these poems, not the more optimistic, Jungian "surrealist" poems, whose music spoke of a daimonic energy in the self, a thrashing sweetness and rage:

> O to break loose, like the chinook
> salmon jumping and falling back,
> nosing up to the impossible
> stone and bone-crushing waterfall—
> raw-jawed, weak-fleshed there, stopped by ten
> steps of the roaring ladder, and then
> to clear the top on the last try,
> alive enough to spawn and die.

Finally, there was the question of the intellectual life, or, to turn to the second half of my title, of "mere life." While I was trying to write a poetry like Crane's, I had been siphoning off into unsuccessful stories and plays a wish to deal more immediately with people, ideas, situations. At Harvard I became friends with a young poet, Frank Bidart, who wanted poetry to go beyond even Lowell's need for the imagistic in order to capture the bareness (as Frank experienced it) of the mind's internal confrontations with itself and life. Talking after Lowell's class, Frank and I would find ourselves at one in what we disliked—all that lukewarm "rendering"—but would stare in antipodean fascinated bewilderment at what each other really wanted from poetry. And yet, as Frank's work has developed, his desire to invent a typography that would capture the exact intonations and hesitations of the internal monologue has been in its own way a foregrounding of the sensuous body of language. And in the lines from "Golden State" from which I take the second half of my title, when the speaker, after all his reasonings and abstractions, looks at the photographs of his father and:

they stare back at me
with the dazzling, impenetrable glitter of mere life

he seems to acknowledge, not only that life resists the impulse toward naked truth, but that in that very resistance there is a "dazzle" which can be the source of another ideal for art. I learned a great deal from Bidart, as well as from Lowell, about the qualities of voice and straightforwardness that could make the material of my unsuccessful stories part of my poetry; and he too was to learn his own way to a very traditional kind of eloquence and splendor.

I do not mean to suggest anything so uniform as a generational style. The norm of magazine verse, certainly, remains a lowest common denominator of the kind of dutiful imagistic "rendering" Frank and I found oppressive and the American surrealists' indifference to sound and the line. (I mean, here, the second-generation "surrealists" attacked in Robert Pinsky's *The Situation of Poetry;* not Wright and Merwin, who are masters of sound, or Kinnell, who is a significant innovator in lineation.) But magazine verse is not likely to represent any period at its best. The poets who give me a sense of generation are those who have somehow reconquered the eloquence, beauty, cultural reach which was "Baudelaire" for Corn, "Hart Crane" for me, and yet have not lost touch with the strong narrative and colloquial way of including "mere life" that was the great acquisition of Lowell's generation. They have also, I think, found available to them a kind of ruminative largeness that did not come easily either to Lowell's generation or to Bly's, perhaps because of the then too immediate, and too formidable, precedents of late Eliot and late Stevens.

What I mean by ruminative largeness may be clearer with the help of another example, from a poet I have not discussed thus far. In the best poems in *History of My Heart*, Robert Pinsky has invented a capacious and almost visionary mixed mode, including but transcending his earlier spirited defense of the "discursive" in poetry. "The Living"—one of my favorites of these poems—begins on a note of magisterial, almost allegorical, generality, shot through with dreamlike, confused processions, surrealist half-visualizations:

The living, the unfallen lords of life,
Move heavily through the dazzle
Where all things shift, glitter or swim—

As on a day at the beach, or under
The stark, absolute blue of a snow morning,
With concentric peals of brightness

Ringing in the cold air.

With the second stanza, this rises to the kind of synaesthetic *correspondence* by which Baudelaire and Rimbaud aspired to capture moments of wordless illumination, to "write down silences, nights, vertigos." It also makes a fine, subtle use of one of the glories of Elizabethan poetry, Nashe's "Brightness falls from the air / Queens have died young and fair." What troubles (but also perhaps enables Pinsky to use and revitalize) this splendor is the sense that it is also a burden, the burden of Being under which we "move heavily" and perceive nothing clearly. Later in the poem, this emotion receives a sharp and sudden narrative correlative. Trying to help a woman who has had a seizure in a supermarket, the speaker feels himself blunderingly forced into the kind of cosmic comedy the opening lines suggest, "acting the part / Of a stranger helping." To make matters worse, the woman, in her own confused perception, and having no one else to blame, seems to blame her rescuer:

As if I had made her fall: or were no
Stranger at all but a son, lover, lord
And master who had thus humiliated her

And now, tucking the blanket around her,
Hypocritical automaton, pretended
To urge—as if without complicity or shame

Or least sense of betrayal—the old embrace
Of this impenetrable haze, this prolonged
But not infinite surfeit of glory.

And, the speaker seems to conclude, the woman is in some way right. For his "embrace" comes to stand for the equally paradoxical "old embrace" of life itself, at once too much and not enough, *la tendre indifférence du monde,* in Camus's unforgettable phrase. The poem rises wonderfully from the norm of intelligent conversation Pinsky defends in his prose to a conclusion which, while abstract and philosophical, draws on the energies both of narrative and of the synaesthetic visionary moment: the definition of life as "this prolonged / But not infinite surfeit of glory," with "surfeit" standing for the nausea of sudden illness, "glory" for the "brightness / Ringing in the cold air."

Pinsky could have framed the incident in the supermarket as a narrative poem in the manner of Frost, or, with a more subjective emphasis, of Lowell. That he did not—but preferred to set it in montage-like relation at once to a poetry of statement and to a poetry of vision—makes him typical of poets his age at their most ambitious and inventive. As Frank Bidart has grown older, his increasingly philosophical bent has allowed him to refigure old "confessional" material—himself and his mother—in terms of St. Augustine and St. Monica, and to merge his own inimitable, earnest, halting voice with the eloquence of mystical discourse:

> *We are not our own source,—*
>
> > *even those of us*
>
> *who made ourselves, creatures*
> *of the Will, the Mirror, and the Dream,*
>
> *know we are not our own source*

And Alfred Corn, near the end of *Notes from a Child of Paradise,* represents his former wife speaking to him in terms which—while far from Jeanne Duval and her cat—legitimately recall the high moments of the Provençal and Dantean vision of love as an education of the spirit:

> "You say you hear me speak and when you do
> From everywhere meaning comes riding in—mine,
> In your invention—addressed, in any case, to you.

Maybe we are still much as we were then.
Remember how, the laundry done, we'd take
A clean, still-warm sheet? And clasping the corners

Advance until our foreheads almost met,
Join hands, let go, and back away again;
Then halve the rectangle and both step forward

To meet again, perhaps this time to kiss; and part
With one left behind to make a final fold,
The soft octavo volume safely shelved. . . .

    I have chosen these four poets somewhat at random; I could have chosen at least ten others, around my age or a little younger, and I am not implying any hierarchy of merit. What these poets have in common is a kind of Romantic or Symbolist vocabulary of fundamental conditions of spirit—but one which does not interfere with the flexibility of those demotic, discursive, or narrative models for poetry that descend so richly from the preceding generations. There are precedents for such a mixture of modes in recent American poetry, but perhaps there are clearer ones in other traditions—not the wilder, but tonally more monotonous, Surrealism that seemed the one thing needed a generation back, but such intense and inward, but partially narrative, works as Montale's Clizia poems, Tsvetayeva's "Poem of the Mountain," Tranströmer's "Baltics." Perhaps recent poets are filling in something that never quite happened in our tradition, because of the anti-Romanticism in American Modernism (and even in Lowell and his contemporaries), and then the total reaction in favor of an archetypal kind of inwardness in the 1960s. Or never happened, at any rate, in its full, suave, mature range of possibilities. It will not suit all temperaments, or fit received definitions of what an avant-garde should be; but to me it is a more beautiful, and a more adequate, poetry, for the full mysteriousness of the self moving through the world.

Index

UNDER DISCUSSION
Donald Hall, General Editor

Volumes in the Under Discussion series collect reviews and essays about individual poets. The series is concerned with contemporary American and English poets about whom the consensus has not yet been formed and the final vote has not been taken. Titles in the series include:

Please write for further information on available editions and current prices.

Ann Arbor   The University of Michigan Press

Printed and bound by CPI Group (UK) Ltd, Croydon, CR0 4YY

13/04/2025

14656507-0002